The Witches Almanac

Spring 2012 — Spring 2013

CONTAINING pictorial and explicit delineations of the
magical phases of the Moon together with information about astrological
portents of the year to come and various aspects of occult knowledge
enabling all who read to improve their lives in the old manner.

The Witches' Almanac, Ltd.

Publishers   Providence, Rhode Island
www.TheWitchesAlmanac.com

Address all inquiries and information to
THE WITCHES' ALMANAC, LTD.
P.O. Box 1292
Newport, RI   02840-9998

10-ISBN: 0-9824323-6-4
13-ISBN: 978-0-9824323-6-5

ISSN: 1522-3183

First Printing August 2011

Printed in Canada

Printed on 97% recycled paper

Established 1971 by Elizabeth Pepper

Preface

MOTHER NATURE can be fearsome.

Have we opened the Pandora's box of nature? Did our race ignore the messages that were sent to us from the environment? Why are we suffering the pains of global climatic change and when will it end? As pressing as these questions may be, they do not spell out total doom for mankind. Change is an inevitable part of being human.

When we are in touch with the natural cycles, we know that seldom do changes occur abruptly, but rather happen over the course of time, much like the changes in our bodies or minds. Our earth is changing. Scientists will tell us that global warming, pollution, solar flares, and abuse of our planet have caused the significant environmental and climatic disruptions that we have seen in recent years. Look around you – unprecedented numbers of tornados in southern U.S., fires in Moscow, hurricanes in the Gulf of Mexico, global earthquakes, tsunami threats, droughts in Russia, and flooding in Australia, China, Pakistan, and central U.S.

As our planet and solar system approach a cosmic alignment with the galactic center, we will see other changes. Many of these will be visible, but many will be invisible – changes in the subconscious of the races, both human and non-human. Just as with an eclipse, there is great opportunity during a time of transformation. Hold fast to your convictions and principles. As our world goes through its renovation, we who remain true to ourselves and the greater good shall emerge in a more peaceful place.

❧ HOLIDAYS ❧

Spring 2012 to Spring 2013

March 20 . . . . .Vernal Equinox
April 1 . . . . All Fools' Day
April 30 . . . . Walpurgis Night
May 1 . . . . Beltane
May 5 . . . . .Vesak Day
May 8 . . . . White Lotus Day
May 9, 11, 13 . . . . Lemuria
May 29 . . . . .Oak Apple Day
June 5 . . . . .Night of the Watchers
June 21 . . . . .Summer Solstice
June 24 . . . . Midsummer
July 23 . . . . Ancient Egyptian New Year
July 31 . . . . Lughnassad Eve
August 1 . . . . Lammas
August 13 . . . . Diana's Day
September 19 . . . . Ganesh Festival
September 23 . . . . Autumnal Equinox
October 31 . . . . .Samhain Eve
November 1 . . . . Hallowmas
November 16 . . . . .Hecate Night
December 17 . . . . Saturnalia
December 21 . . . . Winter Solstice
January 9 . . . . .Feast of Janus
February 1 . . . . .Oimelc Eve
February 2 . . . . Candlemas
February 15 . . . . .Lupercalia
March 1 . . . . Matronalia
March 19 . . . . Minerva's Day

Art Director . . . . Karen Marks

Astrologer . . . . Dikki-Jo Mullen

Climatologist . . . . Tom C. Lang

Cover Art and Design. . .Ogmios MacMerlin

Production Consultant . . . . . . .Robin Antoni

Sales . . . . .Ellen Lynch

Shipping, Bookkeeping . . . . .D. Bullock

ANDREW THEITIC
Executive Editor

JEAN MARIE WALSH
Associate Editor

JUDIKA ILLES
Copy Editor

Contents

A Poison Tree

I was angry with my friend:
I told my wrath, my wrath did end.
I was angry with my foe:
I told it not, my wrath did grow.

And I watered it in fears
Night and morning with my tears,
And I sunned it with smiles
And with soft deceitful wiles.

And it grew both day and night,
Till it bore an apple bright,
And my foe beheld it shine,
And he knew that it was mine,

And into my garden stole
When the night had veiled the pole;
In the morning, glad, I see
My foe outstretched beneath the tree.

— WILLIAM BLAKE

Yesterday, Today and Tomorrow

by Judith Joyce

ELECTRIC LADY. Edith, a very high energy Aries, has always had a strange relationship with electricity. Most people have had the occasional street light go out, but that's small potatoes for Edith, who has blown out household light bulbs by the hundreds. She turns on and off the TV without the remote and has broken hospital equipment and jammed electric doors. In Edith's presence, microwaves start smoking, coffee pots go haywire, watches don't keep accurate time and, well, you get the drift... These occurrences usually happen when she is upset or angry. Friends won't ride in elevators or on planes with Edith. The four lights in the basement go out so often – all at the same time! – that Edith habitually carries a flashlight with her when she goes down to the washing machine. She has been known to turn the TV on and off by crossing and uncrossing her legs from across the room; others sitting in the same place have no effect. Needless to say, Edith owns a lot of flashlights, and she always has batteries on her shopping list.

DOLPHIN VIGILANCE. The celebratory 2011 Fourth of July holiday turned tragic for Luis Arturo Polanco Morales, a 47 year-old resident of Denham Springs, Louisiana, who drowned in Grand Isle. Morales was fishing on the rocks with another man and a young girl. When the girl fell into the water, the men jumped in to rescue her. The other man and the girl were able to make it out of the water alive, but Morales was swept away by the current. His body was later discovered on the shore, where, witnesses reported, it had been brought by dolphins. "They're keeping an eye on us," said an observer, as reported by The Fortean Times.

DO JELLYFISH HATE NUCLEAR POWER? Jellyfish have disabled dozens of nuclear power plants, as far afield from each other as Japan, Israel, and Scotland. These denizens of the deep can also wreak havoc on desalination plants. Jellyfish populations are reputedly on the rise – ocean acidification and global

warming are apparently beneficial for these free-swimming members of the aquatic *Cnidaria* family, also known as Sea Jellies and Medusas. Nuclear and desalination plants draw water from the ocean and possess filtration devices specifically intended to protect against jellyfish and miscellaneous sea debris. These are effective against small numbers of jellyfish, but when their numbers increase, jellyfish can overwhelm and clog these filters. Plant closures are temporary, but with an anticipated jellyfish baby boom, more frequent incidents are expected.

LIGHTNING AND LUCY THE ELEPHANT. Who says lightning doesn't strike twice? Not Lucy the Elephant of Margate, New Jersey, who has been struck by lightning twice: once in 2006 and again in July 2011, mere weeks before Lucy's 130th birthday. That's right, 130. Lucy is not a living, breathing flesh-and-blood pachyderm, but a six-story wood and metal construction. Lucy is a classic example of novelty architecture – she is a building in the form of an elephant. Built in 1882 by Irish-American inventor James V. Lafferty, Lucy, who has been described as the oldest surviving example of zoomorphic architecture, is sixty-five feet tall, sixty-feet long, and weighs approximately nine tons. She has served as a restaurant, a tavern, and is now a beloved tourist attraction. Lucy was designated a National Historic Landmark in 1976. After the 2006 hit caused $162,000 worth of repairs, lightning rods were installed and it's theorized that these helped minimize the damage from the second strike. Although repairs from that strike are estimated at between $10,000 and $100,000, the damage wasn't sufficient to hold up Lucy's birthday celebrations.

SPIDER-MAN VILLAIN ON THE LOOSE. Has Curt Connors, the Spider-Man villain known as the Lizard, stepped from the pages of Marvel Comics? Reports from South Carolina suggest that this may be the case. Ever since 1988, the legendary Lizard Man of South Carolina, described as a scaly, seven-foot creature with glowing red eyes and three-fingered hands, has been accused of mauling and ripping apart automobiles. Along with the equally legendary Jersey Devil and West Virginia's Mothman, Lizard Man ranks among cryptozoology's most pursued targets.

PUTIN AS PAUL. A Russian religious sect considers Prime Minister Vladimir Putin to be an avatar of Saint Paul of Tarsus. This all-female sect, reputedly founded in 2007, is now based near the city of Nizhny Novgorod. Its founder and leader, Mother Fotinya, whose name at birth may have been Svetlana Prolova, has been described as a powerful healer. According to her teachings, in a past life-time, Putin was Paul: she draws multiple parallels between the lives of the two men. Paul, she explains, was initially a persecutor of Christians, but later became the spiritual architect of the Christian Church. Similarly, Putin was "not a saint" during his service with the KGB, but, according to Mother Fotinya, "when he became president, the Holy Ghost descended on him." The group possesses what they describe as a miraculous icon of Putin, who is no stranger to adulation. Russians have previously celebrated him with popular songs and brands of vodka, but this is the first report of religious veneration.

TEMPLES OF TANIT. Archaeologists have recently discovered a significant number of Carthaginian temples in the Azores Islands, an archipelago of nine volcanic islands in the North Atlantic Ocean, west of Portugal. These temples, dating back to the fourth century BCE, are dedicated to the goddess Tanit. Monuments excavated include what are described as "in-built sink-shaped carvings" linked to water conduits, apparently for the purpose of libations, as well as a ceremonial tank, and chairs carved into the rocks. The temples are described as large and well-preserved. Meanwhile, historians continue to argue over Tanit's origins, whether she is originally a Phoenician or a Berber (Amazigh) goddess. The sea-faring Phoenicians carried her veneration into Iberia, which is now modern Spain and Portugal. Numerous ruins and statues associated with her have been unearthed. Tanit is a goddess of love and fertility, who has historically been closely associated with astrologers and star-gazers.

HAWAII'S MERRIE MONARCH FESTIVAL. This week-long festival occurs annually in Hilo and is dedicated to the memory of Hawaii's King David Kalakaua, popularly known as the Merrie Monarch. King David ascended Hawaii's throne in 1874, during an era when what is now America's fiftieth

state was still an independent kingdom. He ruled until his death in 1891. King David restored Hawaiian cultural traditions such as hula, huna, and traditional medicine that had been suppressed by missionaries, thus earning the love of many Hawaiians. The Merrie Monarch Festival, begun in 1964 by the Hawaiian Chamber of Commerce, celebrates traditional Hawaiian culture, especially hula. It features art exhibits, craft fairs, demonstrations, and a three-day long hula competition that draws participants and observers from around the world. Proceeds from the festival are returned back to the community, used to sponsor seminars, workshops, symposiums, and educational scholarships devoted to ancient Hawaiian spiritual arts, as well as the continuation of the Merrie Monarch Festival.

VENOM OR POISON? According to a tradition dating back over two-thousand years, Cleopatra, Egypt's last pharaoh, committed suicide by inducing a snake to bite her in 30 BCE, after her military defeat at the Battle of Actium. Cleopatra's dramatic death has long been a favorite theme of artists: she is typically portrayed grasping an asp – a venomous Egyptian cobra. A new study suggests, however, that this legend is incorrect – that Cleopatra's suicide was caused instead by a sophisticated poison cocktail. Two centuries after her death, Roman historian Cassius Dio wrote that Cleopatra's death was quiet and pain-free, which, according to modern toxicologists and poison specialists does not correspond with the symptoms of an asp's bite, which are painful, disfiguring, unpleasant, and undignified: they include vomiting and diarrhea. Cleopatra's suicide was stimulated by her desperate desire to avoid capture by the Romans: snakes are unpredictable; her death would not have been guaranteed. However, ancient papyri indicate that the Egyptians had a deep and profound knowledge of poisons. Cleopatra, herself, was reputedly an expert on the topic, performing experiments on prisoners in order to test symptoms and rates of fatality. It is now theorized that her death was caused by a plant-based poison cocktail including opium, hemlock, and aconitum (wolfsbane). Historians and toxicologists hope that her remains will soon be discovered, so that these theories can be tested forensically and the mystery solved.

The Locavore Revolution

Nourishing Mind, Body, and Spirit:
Mindful Eating and Going Local

IN 2007, the Oxford American Dictionary named locavore the word of the year, reflecting the growing awareness among Americans of where their food comes from. A "locavore" is defined as one who consumes foodstuffs that are regionally grown or produced as it becomes seasonally available, usually to preserve flavor, strengthen community, and minimize environmental impact. Originally, "regionally grown" meant within a 100-mile radius of your home, but as the popularity of the movement has spread the meaning has become more elastic. Now, self-proclaimed locavores will eat regionally along geographically defined boundaries — mountains or lakes, for instance; limit themselves to food grown domestically; or make the occasional exception to the "local" rule by purchasing specialty items such as chocolate, coffee, tea, wine, or spices. There are many reasons why people become locavores – from political activism to a desire for more nutritious food – but for practitioners of the Old Ways, there are a multitude of unique benefits to "going local."

Preserving Life Force

Locavores often point out that food that must travel great distances over long periods of time is often less nutritionally valuable than food harvested locally and consumed fresh. Local food, they argue, is better for you. Practitioners of the Old Ways may agree but also worry about the loss of life force or vital energy. The minute a fruit is picked its life force begins to diminish. It becomes less and less vital until finally the life force is gone. Food that must travel a great distance is therefore deficient both nutritionally and vitally.

Seasonal Eating and the Wheel of the Year

Practically any and every kind of vegetable and fruit is available to us year round, divorcing us from the knowledge that each food has its season. If apples or zucchini are not currently growing in your region, they are growing in China or Argentina and can thus be shipped to your local supermarket. Not only is this practice bad for the global environment (the average American meal travels 1500 miles, emitting

tons of carbon dioxide and other pollutants along the way), but it also creates a dysfunctional relationship with the Wheel of the Year. Consuming locally grown foods helps you participate in the seasons unfolding around you, not halfway across the globe. Pagans know better than most that all things have their season, and that every ending is a new beginning. Each Sabbat marks both the end and the start of time, an unending, unbroken wheel. Our actions, practices, and rituals help to not only honor our place on this wheel but also to move it forward. Why not have our eating habits do the same thing?

Fortunately, finding locally grown seasonal fruits and vegetables as well as locally produced wares such as cheese, bread and beer is becoming easier as demand grows. Major metropolitan areas as well as smaller cities and towns across the country now host farmers' markets where farmers can sell direct to the community. These markets often have the added benefit of feeding the neediest of the community – unsold stock is usually donated to area food banks. Many supermarket chains have also started offering local fare.

When moving the Wheel along its path, one must look forward. When your local farms are at peak harvest, remember to buy extra large batches of whatever is fresh and cheap to preserve for the long, lean winter months ahead. Canning, jarring, pickling, salting, drying, and freezing are all preservation methods to be considered when looking forward.

Balance in All Things

"Eating seasonally" can go beyond the raw materials ingested to extend to the method of cooking used to prepare them. For example, in the hot summer months one wants to avoid adding yet more heat. One's food should therefore be cooked as little as possible – which shouldn't be a problem considering how many juicy fruits become ripe for picking during these months. Similarly, the cold winter months demand slow-cooked, warm, and hearty foods like soups and breads – easily assembled from frozen veggies and stored grains. In general, hot should be balanced with cold, cold with hot, dry with wet and so forth, so that your meals as well as your energies may achieve balance.

Land Spirits

Nothing says "locavore" more than growing your own food. Cultivating a garden will not only provide you with as much food as you can coax from the soil, but it will also help you cultivate a relationship with your land spirits. These spirits go by many names but no matter what they are called, it is in your best interest to keep them happy. These spirits are closer to you than the

Gods and Goddesses inhabiting the celestial dome and are therefore more likely to cause troublesome mischief if you neglect or abuse them. However, keep them happy and you gain powerful allies who will protect and nurture the tasty fruits (and vegetables!) of your labor.

One way to keep your land spirits happy is to make regular offerings. When you are weeding or watering acknowledge the spirits as you work. Sing them a song of praise and thank them for their help in protecting the garden. Before harvesting acknowledge the role your land spirits played in growing and thank them for it. Remember to give something back to the garden after harvest – return nutrients back to the earth by composting garden and kitchen scraps.

Of course, not everyone has access to land to cultivate. If you find yourself in a city or dense urban area, fear not! There are still plenty of opportunities to commune with the land. There are many innovative ways to garden within a small space. Community gardens allow city dwellers to cultivate their own patch miles from the country. Many farms now offer Community Supported Agriculture programs or CSAs, where people can exchange money or work on the farm for a share of the harvest. Window boxes and window farms (soil-less, hydroponics schemes) can also be employed to grow herbs, lettuce, or edible flowers inside all year long. Whatever your space restrictions, there are opportunities to participate in the cycle of planting, nurturing, and harvesting food.

Bringin' it Home

Becoming a locavore is beneficial in many ways. Locavorism nurtures body, soul, and community – however, it is not always possible to remain a strict locavore. For example, the state of Rhode Island does not produce enough food within the state to feed all of its citizens. If everyone decided to eat local, there would simply not be enough to sustain everyone.

Furthermore, locally produced food tends to be more expensive than what is found in grocery stores, partly because local food reflects the real cost of agriculture while agribusinesses are funded by government subsidies and externalize much of the cost of production. But the practical limits should not destroy the idealistic sentiment of locavorism: that we should all be fully engaged with the food we eat. We should be aware of where our food comes from and who benefits from its consumption. We cannot all be strict locavores, but we can all strive to be more aware of the origins of our food.

– SHANNON MARKS

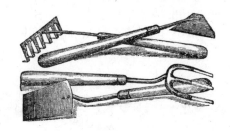

The Magic of Tattoos

TATTOOS. It seems that you see them everywhere now. It was once thought that only delinquents and criminals wore them. But, as we look further back into history, we find evidence of tattooing on every continent, from ancient Egypt to Polynesia, on 2400-year-old mummies in southern Russia, and in cultures throughout the Americas. Otzi – the famous 5300-year-old Alpine mummy – has over 50 tattoos, some on acupressure points that are still in use today. The Inuit of the Alaskan-Canadian Arctic tattoo themselves to protect various parts of the body against disease and to gain strength. In the belief that each joint has a soul, tattoos are applied to help keep the joints strong.

Traditionally, tattooing has been associated with great supernatural powers. In occult practices, it is a means of turning the skin into a living amulet that cannot be lost or stolen. If skin is regarded as a supernatural landscape and sacred geography, then the location of the design becomes crucially important and depends upon the tattoo's intent.

Talismans for Many Purposes

Ancient seamen firmly believed that the words "Hold Fast," tattooed on the knuckles, helped them to literally hold fast to the rigging, thus preventing a fall from aloft. Today, the same spell has been adopted by motorcyclists to help them hold fast to their handlebars – and, possibly, their lives. Just as in times past, modern people, from many cultures, use tattoos as talismans for various purposes. Design and placement of tattoos are intended to alleviate pain, promote well-being, sustain courage, or encourage success. Fertility-related designs remain popular tattoo themes, just as they were in ancient times.

Other tattoos are intended for protection, shielding the inked individual from harm, treachery, or malevolent magick. Some designs are applied to

avert the Evil Eye. One such protective symbol, popular throughout the Mediterranean and Islamic world, is the hand-shaped motif known as the "Hand of Fatima," named after the Prophet Mohammed's favorite daughter. Often depicted with a protective eye, the emblem is also called a *khamsa*, which means "five" in Arabic. This image is believed to provide good fortune as well as protection.

The Ubiquitous, Transcendent Ankh

Symbols such as pentacles, knot-work motifs, and planetary sigils may be employed to symbolize the wearer's devotion to a particular spiritual path, represent a covenant with personal deities, or to aid magic. The ankh, the ancient Egyptian hieroglyph for life, is an example of a symbol that has completely transcended its originating culture and yet is uniquely associated with it. As early as 3000 BCE, the ankh was associated with Imkotep, Egyptian god of medicine and healing. The image of the ankh became ubiquitous, wielded by gods and humans alike.

Not Just for Delinquents Anymore

Today, prejudices and taboos associated with tattooing are fading. There is a certain camaraderie and psychic unity that comes from having a tattoo, and increasing numbers of people from all strata of society are decorating their skin with artwork that is meaningful to them. Tattoos bring the mystique of the past into the present. Thoughtful design and careful placement combine to manifest abstract concepts into physical form, and help anchor our convictions into our lives. Whether it be protective or adventurous, medicinal or spiritual, know your tattoo!

– Nyx Reed

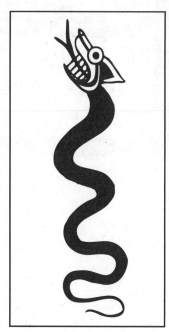

Aubrey Beardsley's illustration for Le Morte d'Arthur, *Dent Edition, 1893-94*

Traces of Paganism in
The Maine Farmer's Almanac
1932-1957

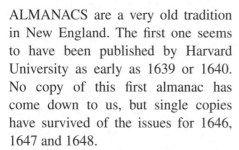

ALMANACS are a very old tradition in New England. The first one seems to have been published by Harvard University as early as 1639 or 1640. No copy of this first almanac has come down to us, but single copies have survived of the issues for 1646, 1647 and 1648.

By the end of the 1600s, several competing almanacs were being published every year in Boston. During the 1700s enterprising printers started rival almanacs in all the other New England states, as well as elsewhere in British North America. The longest-lived of them all, *The Old Farmer's Almanac*, was founded by Robert Bailey Thomas. Its first number was for the year 1793, and it has been going strong ever since. Its most recent issue, for 2011, is the 219th in an unbroken series.

Henry Porter Trefethen

Most of these early New England almanacs were severely practical little booklets, with no more romance in them than is found in a table of logarithms. Their centerpiece was always an astronomical calendar for the coming year. Usually they predicted the weather for the whole year, too. They also included short essays on agriculture, bits of worldly wisdom and local history, the dates of the sittings of the state courts and legislature, lists of the inns along the main roads between cities and towns, and so forth. Occasionally they gave a small nod to astrology in the form of a human figure to show which sign of the zodiac governed which part of the body.

Among them was *The Maine Farmer's Almanac*. Its first number was for the year 1819, edited by Moses Springer Jr. After four years the editorship passed to Daniel Robinson. His name continued to appear on the title page for the next 150 years, although the last *Almanac* that Robinson edited was for 1864. All the later editors published their work anonymously, though

we know who most of these men were from other sources. Until the year 1932, *The Maine Farmer's Almanac* was just as dry and unfanciful as any other almanac published in New England.

Then Henry Porter Trefethen became its editor and things began to change. Not much is known about him as a person, but the 26 numbers of *The Maine Farmer's Almanac* that he edited (for 1932-1957) show him developing a strong interest in Pagan calendar lore and folklore.

Harvest Moon and
Hunter's Moon

He began in a small way. The Almanac for 1932 was no different from earlier numbers. In the Almanac for 1933 he introduced the names Harvest Moon and Hunter's Moon for the full moons in September and October, and he included an essay on Native American names for all the full moons of the year. This essay was signed C.G.F., and thus was not written by Trefethen, but we do not know to whom those initials refer. In the Almanac for 1934, Trefethen included an essay of his own to explain the terms Harvest Moon and Hunter's Moon.

With the Almanac for 1935, Trefethen introduced a complete system of names for all the twelve (or sometimes thirteen) full moons in the year. He also introduced new names for the solstices and equinoxes. In the Almanac for 1943 he also began to mark the cross-quarter days, thereby giving his readers a complete wheel of the year, just as in modern Witchcraft and many forms of Paganism.

At first Trefethen called the cross-quarter days Midwinter, Midspring, Midsummer, and Midautumn. Beginning with the Almanac for 1945, however, they were named Fire Blessing Day, Beltein – Bonfire Day, Fireless Day, and Samthein – Need-fire Day.

The Long Day
and the Long Night

Trefethen named the Winter Solstice Yule, the Long Night. At first, the Summer Solstice was simply called The Long Day in the calendar, though elsewhere in the Almanac for 1935 he referred to it as Lichta, which he said means "day of light." The two equinoxes are called First Day of Spring and Summer's End.

However, in the Almanac for 1945 – the same number in which he first mentioned Beltein and Samthein – he called the Summer Solstice Bael's Day in the calendar. This overt reference to a Pagan God of the Sun must have angered some readers, because the Summer Solstice was left unnamed in the next number of the Almanac (for 1946). Thereafter we hear no more of Bael, but that Solstice is called Aestivum or Estiva (from the Latin word for summer) from 1947 onward.

Trefethen's names of the full moons form a more complicated system. Each of the four seasons normally has three full moons, and they are named in the same way from one year to the next no matter in what month they happen to fall. In its final form, the system of these names is as follows:

	Winter	Spring	Summer	Autumn
First	Yule Moon	Egg Moon	Hay Moon	Harvest Moon
Middle	Wolf Moon	Milk Moon	Grain Moon	Hunter's Moon
Last	Lenten Moon	Honey Moon	Fruit Moon	Ice Moon

Each of these full moons might fall in either of two months, according to how early in the season it occurs. Thus, the Yule Moon might fall either in December or in January, the Wolf Moon in January or February, and so forth.

Now and then a year will have an extra full moon, making thirteen in all. This extra full moon might happen to fall in any of the four seasons, giving that season four full moons instead of its usual three. When that happens, the first, second and last of these four full moons are still named as in the above table, but another name is needed for the third of these four moons. Trefethen consistently called the third full moon in such a season the Blue Moon, probably from the phrase "once in a blue moon," meaning "rarely." This is the very first use anywhere of the term Blue Moon to refer to a specific full moon in the year. (In Trefethen's system, this Blue Moon will never happen to be the second full moon in a month. The common modern use of the term seems first to appear in the game Trivial Pursuit, where it is an error of fact made by the game's designers.)

What moved Henry Porter Trefethen to introduce these Pagan elements into *The Maine Farmer's Almanac*? We have no way of knowing, but we may speculate just a little. The very first Trefethen, Henry Porter's great-great-great-great-great-grandfather, came from Cornwall in England sometime in the 1670s, in the days when Cornish (a Celtic language) was still spoken there. He settled on Great Island (now called New Castle) in New Hampshire. In those early days, Great Island was a very weakly churched part of New England, and the ancestors of several of its leading families did not come from Protestant England, but from more exotic places – one family even came from the Levant. Could Henry Porter Trefethen have been inspired by something he had heard about his early ancestors? Or, perhaps, was he just curious about his own heritage as a Celt? We have no documents that would answer the question for us.

The last Almanac that Trefethen edited was for 1957. Subsequent editors attempted to maintain his complicated system, but did not fully understand how it operated. First there were a few clumsy mistakes in its use, then outright confusion; the last few numbers of the Almanac gave it up altogether. The very last issue of *The Maine Farmer's Almanac*, no. 154, was for the year 1972.

– ROBERT MATHIESEN

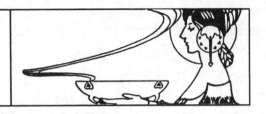

Vanilla

An Exotic History

THE AROMA of vanilla is unmistakable, instantly recognizable, and utterly intoxicating. Vanilla is anything but ordinary and unexciting – it has a history as rich and complex as the spice itself. The ancient Totonaca people of what is now northern Mexico were the first to cultivate the wild vanilla orchid and harvest the exquisite vanilla bean.

Surprisingly, the Totonacans did not grow vanilla to eat. Instead, vanilla was used as an important sacramental fruit and powerful aphrodisiac, with Totonaca maidens weaving the beans in their hair to attract lovers. It was only after the Totonaca people were conquered by the Aztecs that vanilla became an ingredient in cooking. Vanilla was taken back to Tenochtitlan as plunder and combined with chocolate to make a rich drink consumed by Aztec royalty – the first known culinary application of vanilla.

When the Aztecs in turn were conquered by Hernando Cortez, vanilla (along with chocolate) made its way to Spain where it was again enjoyed by royalty in a chocolaty drink.

Amazingly, it would be almost one hundred years before anyone thought to try vanilla independently of chocolate, when Queen Elizabeth I's court chemist suggested vanilla be used as a flavoring all its own. Vanilla has since become a culinary staple with innumerable applications.

Nowadays, most vanilla flavoring in products is actually vanillin, a chemical compound that occurs naturally or can be manufactured in a lab. While similar, vanillin cannot hold a candle to real vanilla. The easiest way to incorporate the sweet intoxicating aroma of genuine vanilla into your own cooking is by making your own extract.

Slit two whole vanilla beans from tip to tip and place them in an 8 ounce dark tinted bottle – the beans can be found in wholesale spice shops or ordered online. Fill the bottle with 80 proof vodka or dark rum. Store in a cool place for three to six months, shaking the bottle weekly. Once ready, your extract can be used in pastries, puddings, and confections of all kinds.

– SHANNON MARKS

Vanilla's Origin

THE ANCIENT Totonaca King Tenitzill III demanded great piety from his subjects, so much so that he decreed even the slightest transgression against the gods punishable by death. Tonacayohua, Mother to All Crops, took notice and rewarded the king, not only with plentiful harvests, but also with a child of unparalleled beauty. Princess Tzacopontziza, or Morning Star, grew to be a maiden of such luminous loveliness that the king resolved that no mortal man was worthy of her. So he gave his daughter to the Temple of Tonacayohua as a living testament to the Goddess' generosity. There, priests raised Morning Star in piety and chastity.

One day, while gathering sacramental flowers in the forest, Morning Star was spotted by a hunter, Zcotan-oxga, or Young Deer. He was immediately intoxicated by her unworldly charm and rushed forward to embrace her, perhaps unaware of the sacrilege he was about to commit. As he wrapped his arms around the Goddess' vassal, a wall of flames surrounded them. When the priests were summoned to witness the guileless lovers' embrace, they beheaded both Young Deer and Morning Star before either could utter a word of defense. Their hearts were carved out and taken back to the temple altar as offerings of appeasement and their bodies left to rot in the forest.

But their bodies did not rot. Perhaps Tonacayohua saw the innocence contained within their still dripping hearts, because Young Deer and Morning Star were allowed to rise from the soil soaked in their blood – Young Deer as a stout bush and Morning Star as the delicate vanilla orchid, her tendrils gently winding up and around Young Deer's strong limbs. As the tiny flowers adorning Morning Star began to open, the entire forest was filled with the erotic sweetness of her scent. The Totonaca people, witness to this miracle, renamed her Xanat, or Hidden Flower, which to this day remains their word for vanilla.

– SHANNON MARKS

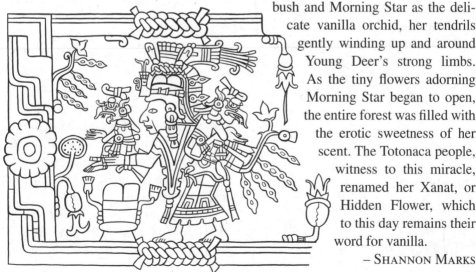

Weather Lore in Rural Pennsylvania

LIKE most contemporary adults, the first thing I do in the morning (well, after turning on the coffee machine) is to check the weather. There are windows in my home – lots of them – but I seldom look outside. Instead I switch on the morning news and wait patiently for the weatherman to tell me how to dress for the day – or if I am in a hurry – I check out the latest cell phone weather "app."

When I was a boy growing up in the mountains of northern Pennsylvania, my mother would typically switch on the radio in the morning. There was only one station available and I think it broadcast from the kitchen of a neighbor's house. When it was time to check the weather, the announcer would say "well, let's open a window and have a look." You'd hear the sound of a creaky window opening and then she would come back and say "yep, it's raining."

Many years later, I was out hiking with a friend and we got turned around in the woods. It was getting late and the sun was about to go down – which is a problem when you're standing in the middle of a pine forest miles from your car. I remember fussing with a compass, trying to find "true west." I was convinced we had to walk toward the west to find the car. My friend started to laugh and I asked what was so funny. She pointed to the sun which was hanging low on the horizon – "Duh, the sun sets in the west."

Fireproof Cows, Singing Bees, and Bushy Tailed Squirrels

Funny how as an adult you think you get smarter. When I was a kid, reading weather signs in nature was always a sure-fire way to tell the difference between "rain or shine." For example, you knew it was going to be a bad winter if the squirrels grew bushy tails or the wooly caterpillars wore a heavy coat. Watch out for lots of snow if the crows gathered in the treetops – presumably they knew it was going to be cold and were getting together to keep warm. Rain was a sure bet if cows laid down in the pasture and watch out for lightning if they gathered under a tree – although standing under a tree in a thunderstorm is not advisable for people, maybe cows are more fireproof?

Another portent of rain was if leaves shook on the trees and showed you their bellies – one particular type of tree

22

is very prone to these anxiety attacks and derives its name from its cowardly actions – the "quaking" aspen. On the other hand, fair weather would prevail if the smoke went straight up out of the chimney or if the bees sang in the orchard.

Groundhog Lore

But perhaps the most well-known Pennsylvanian weather lore was made famous by a movie of the same name: Groundhog Day. This strange local custom occurs every February 2 in Punxsutawney, PA. The annual morning ritual goes like this:

The groundhog emerges from his burrow and takes a look around. If he stays outside, it is winter's end. If he runs back inside, expect eight more weeks of winter.

Considering that the groundhog undoubtedly has to be awakened from his winter nap and forced to go outside on what is typically an unreasonably cold morning, he usually chooses the latter option and high-tails it back inside.

This groundhog lore came to America with the Pennsylvania Dutch but has its origins in 18th century European weather magic when either a badger or bear was the chosen prognosticator – both of which were much grumpier upon being awakened than a groundhog.

In considering that Groundhog Day coincides with the Pagan festival of Imbolg, it seems obvious that the family tree of the most well photographed rodent has Pagan relatives.

However, since many Pennsylvania natives are by nature a conservative and deeply religious folk, any connection to Paganism is denied outright. The mystery of the groundhog is just good old fashioned fun.

Hoodie Hoo Day

This reminds me of a more recent Pennsylvania weather tradition which started years ago in rural mountain towns and is becoming increasingly popular. This, of course, is Hoodie Hoo Day, which occurs every February 20. At precisely twelve noon on this day, Pennsylvania townsfolk throw open their doors and yell three times at the top of their lungs "Hoodie Hoo!" The objective is to raise such a ruckus that Old Man Winter runs for the hills, bringing green grass to the pasture, flowers to the garden, and fruit to the trees. All manner of noise-making is utilized – people sing, stomp, beat on pots and pans, and play loud music. Old ladies and children parade around town in the brightest outfits imaginable. Like the annual ritual with the reluctant groundhog, this is all done in good Christian fun with absolutely no connection to Paganism at all. Yeah, right.

– JIMAHL DI FIOSA

MOON GARDENING

BY PHASE

Sow, transplant, bud and graft		*Plow, cultivate, weed and reap*	

NEW	First Quarter	FULL	Last Quarter	NEW
Plant above-ground crops with outside seeds, flowering annuals.	Plant above-ground crops with inside seeds.	Plant root crops, bulbs, biennials, perennials.		Do not plant.

BY PLACE IN THE ZODIAC

Fruitful Signs

Cancer – Most favorable planting time for all leafy crops bearing fruit above ground. Prune to encourage growth in Cancer.

Scorpio – Second only to Cancer, a Scorpion Moon promises good germination and swift growth. In Scorpio, prune for bud development.

Pisces – Planting in the last of the Watery Triad is especially effective for root growth.

Taurus – The best time to plant root crops is when the Moon is in the sign of the Bull.

Capricorn – The Earthy Goat Moon promotes the growth of rhizomes, bulbs, roots, tubers and stalks. Prune now to strengthen branches.

Libra – Airy Libra may be the least beneficial of the Fruitful Signs, but is excellent for planting flowers and vines.

Barren Signs

Leo – Foremost of the Barren Signs, the Lion Moon is the best time to effectively destroy weeds and pests. Cultivate and till the soil.

Gemini – Harvest in the Airy Twins; gather herbs and roots. Reap when the Moon is in a sign of Air or Fire to assure best storage.

Virgo – Plow, cultivate, and control weeds and pests when the moon is in Virgo.

Sagittarius – Plow and cultivate the soil or harvest under the Archer Moon. Prune now to discourage growth.

Aquarius – This dry sign of Air is perfect for ground cultivation, reaping crops, gathering roots and herbs. It is a good time to destroy weeds and pests.

Aries – Cultivate, weed, and prune to lessen growth. Gather herbs and roots for storage.

Consult our Moon Calendar pages for phase and place in the zodiac circle. The Moon remains in a sign for about two-and-a-half days. Match your gardening activity to the day that follows the Moon's entry into that zodiac sign.

The MOON Calendar

is divided into zodiac signs rather than the more familiar Gregorian calendar.

2012   2013

Bear in mind that new projects should be initiated when the Moon is waxing (from dark to full). When the Moon is on the wane (from full to dark), it is a time for storing energy and the wise person waits.

Please note that Moons are listed by day of entry into each sign. Quarters are marked, but as rising and setting times vary from one region to another, it is advisable to check your local newspaper, library or planetarium.
The Moon's Place is computed for Eastern Standard Time.

We are born at a given moment, in a given place and,
like vintage years of wine, we have the qualities
of the year and of the season of which we are born.
Astrology does not lay claim to anything more.

– *Carl Gustav Jung*

capricorn

December 21 – January 19

Cardinal Sign of Earth ▽ Ruled by Saturn ♄

S	M	T	W	T	F	S
LEAD *Lead and the color black were representative of Saturn's supposed dark and malefic qualities...* – ABC of Magic Charms			DEC. 21 Winter Solstice ❄	22 Sagittarius	23 Store mistletoe	24 ⬤ Capricorn
25 WAXING	26	27 Keep warm Aquarius	28	29 Pablo Casals born, 1876 Pisces	30 Carry a mirror – avoid a curse	31 Aries
JAN. 1 ◑ 2012	2 State year's goals	3 Cicero born, 106 B.C.E. Taurus	4	5 Be patient Gemini	6	7
8 Feast of Janus ⇨ Cancer	9 ◯ Wolf Moon	10 WANING Leo	11	12 Virgo	13 Celebrate	14 Libra
15	16 ◐ Scorpio	17 Wear red for power	18 Sagittarius	19		

4	9	2
3	5	7
8	1	6

Alchemical symbol for lead

The Magic Square of Saturn – nine figures adding up vertically, horizontally, and diagonally to total fifteen – was engraved on a sheet of lead and carried as an amulet. Today lead is often employed as a protective token and used to guard valuables.
– ABC of Magic Charms

⁓ The First Principle ⁓

WHEN ONE GOES to Obaku temple in Kyoto, he sees carved over the gate the words "The First Principle." The letters are unusually large, and those who appreciate calligraphy always admire them as being a masterpiece. They were drawn by Kosen two hundred years ago.

When the master drew them, he did so on paper, from which workmen made the larger carving in wood. As Kosen sketched the letters, a bold pupil was with him who had made several gallons of ink for the calligraphy and who never failed to criticize his master's work.

"That is not good," he told Kosen after the first effort.

"How is that one?"

"Poor. Worse than before," pronounced the pupil.

Kosen patiently wrote one sheet after another, until eighty-four First Principles had been accumulated, still without the approval of the pupil.

Then, when the young man stepped outside for a few moments, Kosen thought: "Now is my chance to escape his keen eye," and he wrote hurriedly, with a mind free from distraction. "The First Principle."

"A masterpiece," pronounced the pupil.

– 101 Zen Tales
edited by NYOGEN SENZAKI

aquarius

January 20 – February 18

Fixed Sign of Air △ Ruled by Uranus ♅

S	M	T	W	T	F	S
SODALITE					Jan. 20	21

SODALITE

This most beautiful stone will fluoresce under ultraviolet light. Darkness will also restore its brilliance, also accelerated by ultraviolet light.

— ABC of Magic Charms

21 — Look toward the future — Capricorn

22

23 — **Year of the Dragon** — Aquarius

24 — WAXING

25 — *Undines are angered* — Pisces

26 — *Eartha Kitt born, 1928*

27

28 — Aries

29

30 — Taurus

31 — *Step on a silver coin*

Feb. 1 — *Oimelc Eve*

2 — Candlemas — Gemini

3 — Contemplate

4 — Cancer

5 — *Melt snow in your hands*

6 — Leo

7 — Storm Moon

8 — WANING — Virgo

9 — *Drink water by moonlight*

10

11 — *Virginia E. Johnson born, 1925* — Libra

12

13 — *Make runes* — Scorpio

14

15 — Lupercalia — Sagittarius

16

17 — *Have a party* — Capricorn

18

Sodalite inspires thoughts as deep as its color and encourages understanding through higher thinking. The stone is excellent for the seeker of wisdom, calming its wearer and promoting deep meditation leading to a balance of thought and spirit.

— ABC of Magic Charms

Love's Secret

Never seek to tell thy love, love that never told can be:
For the gentle wind doth move, silently, invisibly.
— WILLIAM BLAKE

LOVE AND MAGIC are akin. Both arts may be learned but not taught. Neither rely on reason, nor can their power or beauty be readily explained.

Eliphas Levi, the renowned ceremonial magician, listed the rules of the Magus: "TO KNOW, TO DARE, TO WILL, TO KEEP SILENCE." Silence is particularly relevant in love: a tenet of witchcraft holds the act of love to be sacred warning that communication between lovers is often confused by words. "Speak not lest ye break the spell." Other sources echo the same theme. Jaladud-din Rumi, a Persian poet of the 13th century, commented:

"Explanation by the tongue makes most things clear. But love unexplained is better." In our own time, Dorothy Parker, from whom we came to expect more wit than wisdom, said succinctly, "silence is the language of love."

When you find true love (do not settle for less), accord it the awe and respect it deserves. Do not question it or demand in tiresome words the worthless vows so often broken. Love is magic and will live without definition – like the gentle wind, silently, invisibly.

– Originally published in the
1974/1975 Witches' Almanac.

pisces
February 19 – March 20
Mutable Sign of Water ▽ Ruled by Neptune ♆

S	M	T	W	T	F	S
FEB. 19 Aquarius	20 Turn a curse	21 ●	22 WAXING Pisces	23	24 Recite a rhyme Aries	25 Meher Baba born, 1894
26	27 Taurus	28 Leap Year Day ⇨	29 ◑ Gemini	MARCH 1 Matronalia	2 Hold a love's hand Cancer	3 Mix sea, rain and river waters
4	5 Leo	6 Michelangelo born, 1475	7 Spot a rabbit for good luck Virgo	8 Chaste Moon	9 WANING Libra	10
11 Daylight Savings Time begins @ 2am Scorpio	12	13 Stay clear of fires Sagittarius	14 ◑	15 Capricorn	16 Climb a hill	17 Aquarius
18 Read poetry	19 Minerva's Day Pisces	20				

AMETHYST

It was the jewel to the late 10th century worn by the High Priest during the initiation rites into the Eleusinian Mysteries in order that he might not become "confused, distracted or overwhelmed by the intense fascination of external phenomena." The secrets of Eleusis were never revealed, and eventually Dionysos, the god of wine, was worshipped there.

– ABC of Magic Charms

The Lorscher Ring, a dark purple amethyst set in gold is a treasured German antiquity dated to the late 10th century

the Little warrior

A Protective Talisman

IF YOU have a loved one in a war zone or other dangerous area, you can deploy your own little warrior on a mission of protection.

Shops selling Viking artifacts or gaming pieces are a good place to look. There you can find small wooden Viking figurines dressed for battle, a copper or brass gumdrop helmet sitting upon a shock of sheep wool hair. Often one hand holds a spear slightly taller than the warrior, while the other holds a round wooden shield with an iron boss at its center.

Personally, I prefer hand-crafted wooden ones over the modern resin models. If you do, too, and can't find one, you can easily make your own using supplies from a local craft shop. There's an old magickal adage that when you make a thing yourself, you are imbuing it with power.

Here are some suggestions for parts, but use your imagination. If you have a friend who is crafty, ask the friend for suggestions, and even help. As long as you are involved in the making, you are adding your magickal energy.

Head: Round wooden or foam ball

Hair: Lamb's wool or cotton ball

Eyes and nose: Small round wooden bead

Helmet: Aluminum foil or leather

Body: Large wooden thread spool or twig or dowel approximately 3" tall and wide enough to hold the "head"

Arms: Smaller twig or dowel; left arm is only half as long as the right.

Spear: Stiff wire (coat hanger wire will do), thin enough to pass through the hole in the hand

Spearhead: Small triangle of foil or tin or semi-precious stone

Hand: Wooden bead with drilled hole through center

Shield: Round circle of leather or tin

Shield boss: Half-bead

Feet (optional): Black felt

You can achieve a more comical, and therefore warm, effect by having the hair cover the face and making the nose bead poke through the hair.

The Spell

Sit back and think of one aspect of a Viking's code of honor: the enemy of his friend becomes his enemy. Likewise, the friend of his friend becomes a shared loved one.

Name your warrior. Tell him about your loved one's goodness and honor. Tell him that your loved one is now his friend, and that he is now honor-bound to protect your loved one. Allow him to sit at least overnight before taking or sending him to his new friend.

– MORVEN WESTFIELD

aries
March 20 – April 19
Cardinal Sign of Fire △ Ruled by Mars ♂

S	M	T	W	T	F	S
♂		Mar. 20 2012 Vernal Equinox Pisces	21	22 ● Aries	23 WAXING	24
25 Aretha Franklin born, 1942 Taurus	26	27 Keep emotions in check Gemini	28 Plan your garden	29	30 ◑ Cancer	31
April 1 All Fools' Day Leo	2 Tell a joke	3 Virgo	4 Study a new subject	5 Plant flowers tomorrow Libra	6 Seed Moon	7 WANING Scorpio
8	9 Sagittarius	10 Break bad habits	11	12 Till the soil Capricorn	13 ◐	14 Turn the tide Aquarius
15 Show compassion	16 Margot Adler born, 1946 Pisces	17	18 Minerva beckons Aries	19		

MARS

Magnanimous, unconquer'd, boistrous Mars, in darts rejoicing, and in bloody wars; Fierce and untam'd, whose mighty pow'r can make the strongest walls from their foundations shake. – Orphic Hymn to Mars

SIXTY YEARS OF THE MUSEUM OF WITCHCRAFT
A Diamond Jubilee

ON 14 May 2011, England's historic Museum of Witchcraft celebrated its sixtieth anniversary, as well as fifty years at its present location in the village of Boscastle on Cornwall's north coast. This is no small accomplishment, as the Museum has survived fire bombs, decades of abuse from Christian fundamentalists, and the flash floods that swept through Boscastle on 16 August 2004. The Museum of Witchcraft currently houses the world's largest collection of witchcraft-related artifacts and regalia and serves as a showcase, repository, and archive of the magical history of witchcraft.

The brainchild of Cecil Williamson, a brilliant occultist, former film producer, and MI6 agent, the Museum first opened its doors in 1951 in Castletown on the Isle of Man. Gerald Gardner, who is widely considered to be the father of modern Wicca, served as the Museum's resident witch, until he and Williamson had a falling-out.

Over the next ten years, the Museum moved to several locations, with consistently unhappy results, as locals did not welcome a museum devoted to witchcraft. For example, during a brief stay in Bourton-on-the-Water, in the Cotswolds, a local vicar preached against the Museum, which was then fire bombed. Dead cats were hung from trees on its grounds. Finally, in 1961, the Museum found its home in Boscastle, where it remains. Controversy continues, however, and the current owner still receives death threats from those who consider witchcraft to be evil.

Williamson ran the Museum, until – at midnight on Halloween of 1996, three years before his death – he passed his mantle to Graham King, the current director. Under King's careful watch, the Museum continues to flourish and to serve as a precious resource to students of witchcraft and the occult. It is also a tremendous tourist destination: the Museum of Witchcraft attracts visitors from around the globe and its collection has a five-star Trip Advisor rating. Further information may be found at www.museumofwitchcraft.com.

– JUDIKA ILLES

taurus
April 20 – May 19
Fixed Sign of Earth ♉ Ruled by Venus ♀

S	M	T	W	T	F	S
VENUS *Heav'nly, illustrious, laughter-loving queen, sea-born, night-loving, of an awful mien; 'Tis thine the world with harmony to join, for all things spring from thee,* (continued below)					APRIL **20**	**21** Taurus
22 WAXING	**23**	**24** Gemini	**25**	**26** Work in the garden Cancer	**27** Henry Percy born, 1564	**28** Prepare for the feast
29 Leo	**30** Walpurgis Night	MAY **1** Beltane Virgo	**2** Sing and dance	**3** Libra	**4** Vesak Day ⇨	**5** Hare Moon Scorpio
6 WANING	**7** Sagittarius	**8** White Lotus Day	**9** Make honorable decisions Capricorn	**10**	**11** Avoid gossip Aquarius	**12**
13 Record a vision Pisces	**14**	**15**	**16** Defend loved ones Aries	**17**	**18** Comfort pets Taurus	**19** Julius Evolva born, 1898

O pow'r divine. Goddess of marriage, charming to the sight, mother of Loves, whom banquetings delight; Source of persuasion, secret, fav'ring queen, illustrious born, apparent and unseen; Spousal, lupercal, and to men inclin'd, prolific, most-desir'd, life-giving, kind... Come, all-attractive to my pray'r inclin'd, for thee, I call, with holy, reverent mind. – Orphic Hymn to Venus

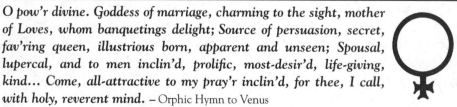

❧ Oak Apple Day, May 29th ❧

His Royal Highness Up a Tree

OAK TREES have been considered sacred since pagan times, but we doubt that King Charles II kept that much in mind as he shinnied upward, fleeing for his life. The king, evading Cromwell's soldiers, took refuge in a lofty, bushy oak, perfect for camouflage. The ruse saved the king's life, and to this day a descendant of that tree is honored as the Royal Oak, its name the third most common in pub signs.

Kings don't usually go in for arbor sports, but Charles was hard pressed, fleeing to Boscobel Castle after defeat at the Battle of Worcester. His hosts cut his fashionably long hair, dressed him in rough clothes, and propelled him upward. Here the king stayed the whole day, fortified by bread, cheese and beer.

The account has all the earmarks of an historical legend. But years later Charles related the details of his arboreal experience to the diarist Samuel Pepys, and so we have the story – including sight of a soldier under the tree as the king was "peeking from the wood." Would a diarist prevaricate?

King Charles escaped and the tree seemed to deserve celebration. In 1660, Parliament declared May 29 Oak Apple Day, and the Royal Oak came to national attention. The tree standing today is not the original, which languished in the nineteenth century, as too many tourists snapped off souvenir leaves, twigs and bark. It has been succeeded by the Son of the Royal Oak, and, a few years ago, Prince Charles planted a sapling grown to the present Grandson of the Royal Oak. English tradition dies hard.

The "apple" referred to a gall resembling the fruit, reddish or brownish, formed on branches by larvae of hornets. In parts of England, where oak apples were known as "shick-shacks," the holiday was also known as Shick-Shack Day. Celebrants wore sprigs of oak, and the royal association also resonates with the pagan tradition of tree worship. But another connection is less lofty. Although Oak Apple Day was abolished in 1859, here and there children still have their own festive ways, although the origin of the holiday has been lost to them. On May 29, they challenge each other to show their oak sprigs. Kids lacking the leafy symbols are fair game for having their bottoms pinched, and the holiday is also termed Pinch Bum Day. Children tend to have a rhyme for every occasion, and so for this peculiar arbor day they chant: "The 29th of May is Oak Apple Day. If you don't give us a holiday, we'll all run away."

– BARBARA STACY

gemini
May 20 – June 20
Mutable Sign of Air ♎ Ruled by Mercury ☿

GEMINI

S	M	T	W	T	F	S
MAY 20 ⬤ Gemini	21 Partial solar ⬅ eclipse WAXING	22 *Sir Arthur Conan Doyle born, 1859*	23 Cancer	24	25	26 Leo
27	28 ◗ Virgo	29 Oak Apple Day	30 *Study tarot* Libra	31	JUNE 1 *Write poetry* Scorpio	2
3 Partial lunar eclipse ⮕ Sagittarius	4 ◯ Dyad Moon	5 WANING Capricorn	6 Night of the Watchers ⬅	7 *Meditate on the stars* Aquarius	8	9
10 *Howlin' Wolf born, 1910* Pisces	11 ◐	12 Aries	13 *Read the clouds*	14 Taurus	15	16 *Converse with the birds*
17 Gemini	18 *Construct a charm*	19 ⬤	20 WAXING Cancer			

ᗰERCURY

With winged feet, 'tis thine thro' air to course, O friend of man, and prophet of discourse: Great life-supporter, to rejoice rejoice is thine, in arts gymnastic, and in fraud divine: With pow'r endu'd all language to explain, of care the loos'ner, and the source of gain. Whose hand contains of blameless peace the rod, Corucian, blessed, profitable God; Of various speech, whose aid in works we find, and in necessities to mortals kind...Assist my works, conclude my life with peace, give graceful speech, and me memory's increase. – Orphic Hymn to Mercury

Notable Quotations

THE SUN

The sun, too, shines into cesspools and is not polluted.

– *Diogenes*

Three things cannot be long hidden: the sun, the moon, and the truth.

– *Buddha*

The sun is new each day.

– *Heraclitus*

Neither the sun nor death can be looked at with a steady eye.

– *Francois de La Rochefoucauld*

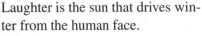

Behold, my friends, the spring is come; the earth has gladly received the embraces of the sun, and we shall soon see the results of their love!

– *Sitting Bull*

Laughter is the sun that drives winter from the human face.

– *Victor Hugo*

Let every dawn be to you as the beginning of life, and every setting sun be to you as its close.

– *John Ruskin*

The sun does not shine for a few trees and flowers, but for the wide world's joy.

– *Henry Ward Beecher*

Mama exhorted her children at every opportunity to 'jump at the sun.' We might not land on the sun, but at least we would get off the ground.

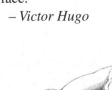

– *Zora Neale Hurston*

The sun, with all those planets revolving around it and dependent on it, can still ripen a bunch of grapes as if it had nothing else in the universe to do.

– *Galileo Galilei*

cancer
June 21 – July 22
Cardinal Sign of Water ▽ Ruled by Moon ☽

S	M	T	W	T	F	S
	MOON *Hear, Goddess queen, diffusing silver light, bull-horn'd and wand'ring thro' the gloom of Night. With stars (continued below)*			JUNE **21** Summer Solstice ☼	**22** Leo	**23** Gather St. John's wort
24 Midsummer Virgo	**25** Gift the Fairies	**26**	**27** Libra	**28** Theodore Reuss born, 1855	**29** Practice water witching Scorpio	**30**
JULY **1** Sagittarius	**2**	**3** Mead Moon Capricorn	**4** WANING	**5** Beware of violent storms Aquarius	**6** Frida Kahlo born, 1907	**7** Create an illusion Pisces
8	**9** Avoid conflict Aries	**10**	**11**	**12** Taurus	**13** Dine with friends	**14** Gemini
15	**16**	**17** Fire has no patience Cancer	**18**	**19**	**20** WAXING Leo	**21**

22 Praise the heavens Virgo

surrounded, and with circuit wide Night's torch extending, thro' the heav'ns you ride. Shine on these sacred rites with prosp'rous rays, and pleas'd accept thy suppliant's mystic praise.
– Orphic Hymn to the Moon

The Rigs O'Barley

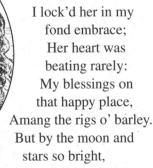

It was upon a
Lammas night,
When corn rigs
are bonie,
Beneath the moon's
unclouded light,
I held awa to Annie;
The time flew by,
wi' tentless heed;
Till, 'tween the late and early,
Wi' sma' persuasion she agreed
To see me thro' the barley

Corn rigs, an' barley rigs,
An' corn rigs are bonie:
I'll ne'er forget that happy night,
Amang the rigs wi' Annie.

The sky was blue, the wind was still,
The moon was shining clearly;
I set her down, wi' right good will,
Amang the rigs o' barley:
I ken't her heart was a' my ain;
I lov'd her most sincerely;
I kiss'd her owre and owre again,
Amang the rigs o' barley.

Corn rigs, an' barley rigs,
An' corn rigs are bonie:
I'll ne'er forget that happy night,
Amang the rigs wi' Annie.

I lock'd her in my
fond embrace;
Her heart was
beating rarely:
My blessings on
that happy place,
Amang the rigs o' barley.
But by the moon and
stars so bright,
That shone that hour so clearly!
She ay shall bless that happy night
Amang the rigs o' barley.

Corn rigs, an' barley rigs,
An' corn rigs are bonie:
I'll ne'er forget that happy night,
Amang the rigs wi' Annie.

I hae been blythe wi' comrades dear;
I hae been merry drinking;
I hae been joyfu' gath'rin gear;
I hae been happy thinking:
But a' the pleasures e'er I saw,
Tho' three times doubl'd fairly –
That happy night was worth them a',
Amang the rigs o' barley.

Corn rigs, an' barley rigs,
An' corn rigs are bonie:
I'll ne'er forget that happy night,
Amang the rigs wi' Annie.

– ROBERT BURNS

leo

July 23 – August 22
Fixed Sign of Fire △ Ruled by Sun ☉

LEO

S	M	T	W	T	F	S
☉	JULY 23 Ancient Egyptian New Year	24 Alexandre Dumas born, 1802 Libra	25	26 Scorpio	27	28 Fly a kite Sagittarius
29 Greet the sunrise	30 Bake bread Capricorn	31 Lughnassad Eve	AUGUST 1 Wort Moon Aquarius	2 Lammas ⇦ WANING	3	4 Barack Obama born, 1961 Pisces
5 Beware of enemies	6 Aries	7	8 Try harder Taurus	9	10	11 See a sign in the clouds Gemini
12 Enjoy a feast	13 Diana's Day Cancer	14	15 Contact an old friend Leo	16	17	18 WAXING Virgo
19	20 Meet a new love Libra	21	22 Enjoy life Scorpio			

SUN

Hear golden Titan, whose eternal eye with broad survey, illumines all the sky. Self-born, unwearied in diffusing light, and to all eyes the mirrour of delight: Lord of the seasons, with thy fiery car and leaping coursers, beaming light from far. – Orphic Hymn to the Sun

The Lion and the Mouse

ONCE, WHEN A LION was asleep, a little Mouse began running up and down upon him; this soon wakened the Lion, who placed his huge paw upon him, and opened his big jaws to swallow him. "Pardon, O King," cried the little Mouse, "forgive me this time, I shall never forget it: who knows but what I may be able to do you a turn some of these days?" The Lion was so tickled at the idea of the Mouse being able to help him, that he lifted up his paw and let him go. Some time after, the Lion was caught in a trap, and the hunters, who desired to carry him alive to the King, tied him to a tree while they went in search of a wagon to carry him on. Just then, the little Mouse happened to pass by, and seeing the sad plight in which the Lion was, went up to him and soon gnawed away the ropes that bound the King of the Beasts. "Was I not right?" said the little Mouse.

MORAL: Little friends may prove great friends.

virgo

August 23 – September 22

Mutable Sign of Earth ▽ Ruled by Mercury ☿

S	M	T	W	T	F	S
VULCAN *Strong, mighty Vulcan, bearing splendid light, unweary'd fire, with flaming torrents bright: Strong-handed, deathless,* (continued below)				AUG. **23** *Gene Kelley born, 1912*	**24** Sagittarius	**25**
26 *Keep silent* Capricorn	**27**	**28**	**29** *Beware of lightning* Aquarius	**30**	**31** ◯ Barley Moon Pisces	SEPT. **1** WANING
2 Aries	**3**	**4** *Burn sweet incense*	**5** Taurus	**6**	**7** *Plan a trip* Gemini	**8** ◑
9 *Understand hidden truths*	**10** *Marie Laveau born, 1794* Cancer	**11** *Bake with corn meal*	**12** Leo	**13** *Save coins*	**14** *Gather seeds* Virgo	**15** ●
16 WAXING Libra	**17**	**18** Scorpio	**19** *Ganesh Festival*	**20** Sagittarius	**21** *Wear a charm of copper*	**22** ◐

and of art divine, pure element, a portion of the world is thine: All-taming artist, all-diffusive pow'r, 'tis thine supreme, all substance to devour… Hear, blessed power, to holy rites incline, and all propitious on the incense shine: Suppress the rage of fires unweary'd frame, and still preserve our nature's vital flame. – Orphic Hymn to Vulcan

The Rose from the Grave of Homer

ALL THE songs of the east speak of the love of the nightingale for the rose in the silent starlight night. The winged songster serenades the fragrant flowers.

Not far from Smyrna, where the merchant drives his loaded camels, proudly arching their long necks as they journey beneath the lofty pines over holy ground, I saw a hedge of roses. The turtle-dove flew among the branches of the tall trees, and as the sunbeams fell upon her wings, they glistened as if they were mother-of-pearl. On the rose-bush grew a flower, more beautiful than them all, and to her the nightingale sung of his woes; but the rose remained silent, not even a dewdrop lay like a tear of sympathy on her leaves. At last she bowed her head over a heap of stones, and said, "Here rests the greatest singer in the world; over his tomb will I spread my fragrance, and on it I will let my leaves fall when the storm scatters them. He who sung of Troy became earth, and from that earth I have sprung. I, a rose from the grave of Homer, am too lofty to bloom for a nightingale." Then the nightingale sung himself to death. A camel-driver came by, with his loaded camels and his black slaves; his little son found the dead bird, and buried the lovely songster in the grave of the great Homer, while the rose trembled in the wind.

The evening came, and the rose wrapped her leaves more closely round her, and dreamed: and this was her dream.

It was a fair sunshiny day; a crowd of strangers drew near who had undertaken a pilgrimage to the grave of Homer. Among the strangers was a minstrel from the north, the home of the clouds and the brilliant lights of the aurora borealis. He plucked the rose and placed it in a book, and carried it away into a distant part of the world, his fatherland. The rose faded with grief, and lay between the leaves of the book, which he opened in his own home, saying, "Here is a rose from the grave of Homer."

Then the flower awoke from her dream, and trembled in the wind. A drop of dew fell from the leaves upon the singer's grave. The sun rose, and the flower bloomed more beautiful than ever. The day was hot, and she was still in her own warm Asia. Then footsteps approached, strangers, such as the rose had seen in her dream, came by, and among them was a poet from the north; he plucked the rose, pressed a kiss upon her fresh mouth, and carried her away to the home of the clouds and the northern lights. Like a mummy, the flower now rests in his *Iliad*, and, as in her dream, she hears him say, as he opens the book, "Here is a rose from the grave of Homer."

– HANS CHRISTIAN ANDERSEN, 1842

libra

September 23 – October 22

Cardinal Sign of Air ♎ Ruled by Venus ♀

LIBRA

S	M	T	W	T	F	S
SEPT. 23 Autumnal Equinox ♌ Capricorn	**24**	**25** Aliens inquire Aquarius	**26** George Gershwin born, 1898	**27** Pisces	**28**	**29** ◯ Blood Moon Aries
30 WANING	**OCT. 1**	**2** Bless seeds Taurus	**3**	**4** Listen to music Gemini	**5** Guido von List born, 1848	**6** Plant bulbs Cancer
7	**8** ◑ Leo	**9**	**10** Dress with style	**11**	**12** Forgive a friend Virgo	**13**
14 Don't disturb the ghosts Libra	**15** ● 	**16** WAXING Scorpio	**17**	**18** Time to travel Sagittarius	**19**	**20** Spirits whisper secrets Capricorn
21 ◑	**22** Enjoy a chance meeting Aquarius					

STARS

With holy voice I call the stars on high, pure sacred lights and genii of the sky. Celestial stars, the progeny of Night, in whirling circles beaming far your light, Refulgent rays around the heav'ns ye throw, eternal fires, the source of all below.

With flames significant of Fate ye shine, and aptly rule for men a path divine... Hail twinkling, joyful, ever wakeful fires! Propitious shine on all my just desires; These sacred rites regard with conscious rays, and end our works devoted to your praise. – Orphic Hymn to the Stars

A Séance Invocation

There is a land where we all go,
Whence ne'r the frost nor cold wind blow,
And friends remembered reunite,
And those who hate, forget their spite.
In glow surround these gentle beings,
We call you now to bless our meetings,
Heaven's promise, our spirits thrive,
So now for the living, let the dead come alive.
Greetings Spirits… Speak thee to us?

– from The Spirit Speaks
Weekly Newspaper, 1901

Ghost Friendly Lavender, Flowers and Music

LAVENDER IS KNOWN to attract spirits. A dish of lavender flower clusters, either dried or fresh, is an invaluable aid for the medium in the séance room. Lavender will relieve depression or negativity and heighten spirituality.

A traditional Victorian séance is held by candlelight. When the candle flame turns blue, a ghost is present. Fresh flowers for the table and music are other helpful elements to ensure a successful séance.

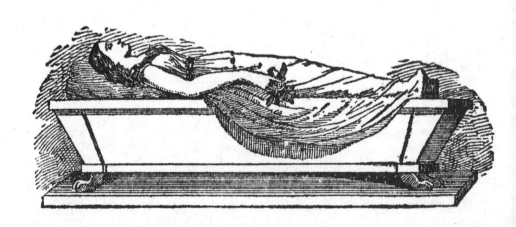

scorpio
October 23 – November 21
Fixed Sign of Water ▽ Ruled by Pluto ♀

SCORPIVS

S	M	T	W	T	F	S
♇		Oct. 23 Revisit family photographs	24 Pisces	25 Wear a mask	26 Constant Chevillon born, 1880	27 Honor ancestors Aries
28	29 Snow Moon Taurus	30 WANING	31 Samhain Eve	Nov. 1 Hallowmas Gemini	2 Visit a cemetery	3 Benvenuto Cellini born, 1500 Cancer
4 Daylight Savings Time ends @ 2am	5	6 Leo	7 Travel by night	8 Scatter patchouly seeds Virgo	9	10 Record your dreams Libra
11 Beware of a curse	12 Total solar eclipse ⇨ Scorpio	13	14 WAXING Sagittarius	15 Wear dark purple for vision	16 Hecate Night Capricorn	17 Cleanse your home
18 Honor Theo tonight Aquarius	19	20	21 Burn sage Pisces			

pluto

Pluto, magnanimous, whose realms profound are fix'd beneath the firm and solid ground, in the Tartarian plains remote from fight, and wrapt forever in the depths of night; Terrestrial Jove, thy sacred ear incline, and, pleas'd, accept thy mystic's hymn divine. Earth's keys to thee, illustrious king belong, its secret gates unlocking, deep and strong… O pow'r all-ruling, holy, honor'd light, thee sacred poets and their hymns delight: Propitious to thy mystic's works incline, rejoicing come, for holy rites are thine. –Orphic Hymn to Pluto

Obsience to Her
Who is Pure Being, Consciousness, Bliss.
As Power,
Who Exists in the Forms of Time and Space,
And All That is Therein,
Who is the Divine Illuminatrix in All Beings.
                    — A TANTRIC PRAYER

sagittarius

November 22 – December 20

Mutable Sign of Fire △ Ruled by Jupiter ♃

S	M	T	W	T	F	S
JUPITER *O Jove much-honor'd, Jove supremely great, to thee our holy rites we consecrate... The earth is* (continued below)				Nov. 22	23 Burn juniper Aries	24
25 Taurus	26 *Prepare for the eclipse*	27 *Partial lunar eclipse* ⇨	28 (Oak Moon) Gemini	29 WANING	30 *Jonathan Swift born, 1667* Cancer	Dec. 1
2 *Practice a spell*	3 Leo	4	5 *Wish upon a cloud* Virgo	6 ◑	7	8 *Jack Frost visits early* Libra
9 *John Milton born, 1608*	10 *Beware the Vampyre* Scorpio	11	12 *See the future* Sagittarius	13 ●	14 WAXING Capricorn	15
16 *Fairy Queen Eve* Aquarius	17 *Saturnalia*	18 Pisces	19 *Meditate*	20 ◐	♃	

thine, and mountains swelling high, the sea profound, and all within the sky...
Ev'n Nature trembles at thy mighty nod, loud-sounding, arm'd with light'ning,
thund'ring God. Source of abundance, purifying king, O various-form'd from
whom all natures spring; Propitious hear my pray'r, give blameless health, with
peace divine, and necessary wealth. – Orphic Hymn to Jupiter

Hymn to Lucifer

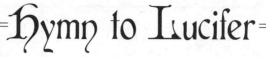

Andante

Jera Runesinger

Lord of the new-born day fill my heart with cou-rage joy and might. Lord of the liv-ing flame fill my heart with ra-diant sun light. Shine forth in all I see. Shine forth in all that I may do. Lord of the new-born day help me grow to be more like you.

Go to www.TheWitchesAlmanac.com/AlmanacExtras/
to hear this song sung by the composer.

capricorn

December 21 – January 19
Cardinal Sign of Earth ▽ Ruled by Saturn ♄

S	M	T	W	T	F	S
♄ **SATURN** *Etherial father, mighty Titan, hear, great fire of Gods and men, whom all revere: Endu'd with various council, pure and strong, to whom perfection and decrease belong.* (continued below)					DEC. **21** Winter Solstice ❄ Aries	**22** Plan a new life
23 Gather personal strength Taurus	**24**	**25** Carlos Casteneda born, 1925 Gemini	**26** Bide your time	**27** Pray to the moon	**28** ◯ Wolf Moon Cancer	**29** WANING
30 Leo	**31** Consult an oracle	JAN. **1** 2013	**2** Buy a coconut Virgo	**3**	**4** ◑ Libra	**5** Stress lessens
6 Dismiss doubt Scorpio	**7**	**8** Sagittarius	**9** Feast of Janus	**10** Brew a strong tea Capricorn	**11** ●	**12** WAXING Aquarius
13	**14** Toss a coin three times Pisces	**15**	**16** Carry bloodstone Aries	**17** Robert Fludd born, 1637	**18** ◐	**19** Don't be stubborn Taurus

Consum'd by thee all forms that hourly die, by thee restor'd, their former place supply... No parts peculiar can thy pow'r enclose, diffus'd thro' all, from which the world arose, O, best of beings, of a subtle mind, propitious hear to holy pray'rs inclin'd; The sacred rites benevolent attend, and grant a blameless life, a blessed end. – Orphic Hymn to Saturn

Willow

Saille

WILLOWS are magical trees with slender pale silver-green leaves. The weeping willow originated in China, where it graced cemeteries as a symbol of immortality, and the tree had spread to the Near East by Biblical times. An Old Testament reference to the exiled Jews hanging their harps upon the willows as they wept beside the rivers of Babylon led to the weeping willow's classification by Linnaeus as *Silax babylonica*. In ancient Greece, the goddess Hera was born under a willow on the island of Samos, where a magnificent temple was guilt to honor her. In the underworld kingdom of Pluto and Persephone, Orpheus touched a willow branch and received the gift of supernatural eloquence. Willow groves are sacred to Hecate, dark goddess of witchcraft.

During the Middle Ages, the willow became a traditional motif adorning tombs. Early 19th-century gravestones throughout New England were decorated with the willow emblem.

An old spell uses a willow to dismiss love and transform passion into friendship: *At Full Moon snip a foot-long tendril from a weeping willow tree and braid it with equal lengths of bright red and cool green yarn. Tie three knots in the braid and hang the charm in an airy room until the Moon is in its last quarter. On three successive nights untie the knots one by one in privacy and silence while concentrating on your desire. Before the New Moon rises, burn the red strand to ashes and throw to the winds. Coil the willow and green wool together and place in an envelope for safe-keeping.*

The willow of the Druids was not the weeping willow, but the tree or shrub we know as the pussy willow. The Irish called the pussy willow one of the "seven noble trees of the land."

The pussy willow is used in love charms as a guard against evil and its wands are often employed in divination. Reflecting the ancient status of the pussy willow, it is the wood to "knock on" and avert bad luck.

Medieval herbalists placed all willows under the rulership of the moon.

aquarius

January 20 – February 18
Fixed Sign of Air ♎ Ruled by Uranus ♅

S	M	T	W	T	F	S
Jan. 20	21 Gemini	22	23 Raise a storm	24 Cancer	25 Gather in a circle	26 (Storm Moon) Leo
27 WANING	28	29 Johann Reuchlin born, 1455 Virgo	30 Prepare for the Sabbat	31 Oimelc Eve Libra	Feb. 1 Candlemas	2 Light a red candle Scorpio
3 ◑	4 Light a white candle	5 Honor Oya Sagittarius	6	7 Capricorn	8 Evangeline Adams born, 1868	9 Fortune smiles Aquarius
10 	11 WAXING Pisces	12	13 Act with caution Aries	14	15 Lupercalia Taurus	16 Live, laugh, love
17 ●	18 Speak freely Gemini					

⊢⊢

URANUS

Great Heav'n, whose mighty frame no respite knows, father of all, from whom the world arose: Hear, bounteous parent, source and end of all, forever whirling round this earthly ball; Abode of Gods, whose guardian pow'r surrounds th' eternal World with ever during bounds; Whose ample bosom and encircling folds the dire necessity of nature holds. Æthereal, earthly, whose all-various frame azure and full of forms, no power can tame. All-seeing Heav'n, progenitor of Time, forever blessed, deity sublime, Propitious on a novel mystic shine, and crown his wishes with a life divine. – Orphic Hymn to Uranus

Sacred Prayer Cloths

FROM MAGIC carpets to saris, handkerchiefs, aprons, altar cloths, keepsake quilts and baby shawls, special fabrics have long been used to carry energy and encouragement to those in need. These fabric talismans are collectively called 'prayer cloths' among the wise witches who use them to heal. Patients in nursing homes and hospitals often appreciate and find solace in gifts of prayer cloths, often with a drop of essential oil or a bit of ribbon or lace added. In 2005, a group of well-wishers even started to send prayer cloths to the United States military troops stationed overseas. Soldiers found comfort in placing squares of cloth inside a pocket or helmet as a kind of talisman. The Masons wear ritual aprons which signify power too.

According to the New Testament's Acts 19:11-12: "God wrought special miracles by the hands of Paul; so that from his body were brought unto the sick handkerchiefs or aprons, and the diseases departed from them, and the evil spirits went out of them." This describes how cloths, specifically aprons and handkerchiefs touched by the apostle Paul were brought back to the sick in order to cure them of their ills.

Prayer cloths are sacred keepsakes in themselves but can also be used with crystals, pictures and other sacred and holy objects. In many places, the custom exists to place the prayer cloth on a special table and to place petitions on top, as well as pictures of our loved ones and those in need of spiritual or physical healing. The prayer cloth may also be placed under a pillow at night or held while praying. Prayer cloths can be used for all kinds of cures, as aids for loneliness, consolation, family difficulties, and various calamities, as well as to enhance special occasions, and devotional praying. A handcrafted handkerchief, perhaps decorated with crocheted lace may be included in greeting cards or given as a gift to send healing to an ill friend or relative in the hospital.

To create a prayer cloth, carefully select a piece of fabric which is special to you. Hold it in your hands and focus on healing as you say a favorite prayer or affirmation. Your cloth may be further empowered by bringing it to sacred places, touching it to crystals, religious icons, angel statues, family photos or other sacred objects.

Many miracles and healings have been attributed to sacred fabrics over the centuries. Simply place the cloth on any part of the body which needs healing or use it on an animal companion who isn't feeling well. Don't be surprised if you experience amazing results!

– ESTHER ELAYNE

pisces

February 19 – March 20

Mutable Sign of Water ▽ Ruled by Neptune ♆

S	M	T	W	T	F	S
		Feb. 19	20 *Exercise caution* Cancer	21	22 *Love with all your being*	23 Leo
24 *Look for a mermaid tomorrow*	25 Chaste Moon Virgo	26 WANING	27 *Consider an alternative* Libra	28 *Moina Mathers born, 1865*	March 1 Matronalia	2 Scorpio
3	4 Sagittarius	5 *Trust an omen*	6 *Be specific* Capricorn	7	8 Aquarius	9 *Teach sorcery*
10 *Daylight Savings Time begins @ 2am* Pisces	11	12 WAXING Aries	13 *Use hypnosis*	14 *Algernon Blackwood born, 1869*	15 Taurus	16 *Eat something sweet*
17 *Read poetry* Gemini	18 Minerva's Day ⇨	19	20 Cancer			

NEPTUNE

Hear, Neptune, ruler of the sea profound, whose liquid grasp begirts the solid ground... Thy awful hand the brazen trident bears, and ocean's utmost bound, thy will reveres: Thee I invoke, whose steeds the foam divide, from whose dark locks the briny waters glide; Whose voice loud founding thro' the roaring deep, drives all its billows, in a raging heap; When fiercely riding thro' the boiling sea, thy hoarse command the trembling waves obey. – Orphic Hymn to Neptune

Origins of the Mithras Cult

A Glimpse of Mystery

THE MYSTERIOUS cult of Mithras – a secret initiatory religion – spread like wildfire through Roman-occupied territories. Although the many inscriptions found among votive offerings attest that Mithras was primarily a soldier's deity, the ideals of truth, light, and might associated with him were sufficient to spur even the less martially-minded to seek initiation into the Mithraic mysteries. Metropolitan areas became so rife with his worship that early Christian writers like Tertullian and Augustine wrote scathing essays intended to vilify the deity that had captured so many hearts.

Virtually no literature regarding this syncretic god survives. Apart from the occasional mention in Graeco-Egyptian magical papyri, the only written accounts of his rites derive from contemporary – but uninitiated – Pagan philosophers like Emperor Julian and the Neo-Platonist Porphyry, or from hostile Christian detractors. Thus, it is the occult iconography of Mithraic temples that historians analyze, fervently seeking to comprehend and explain complex rites of initiation and worship.

All-Seeing, All-Knowing and Forever Just

The earliest documented mention of "Mitra" is in a treaty between the Hittites and the Mitanni, from approximately the 14th century BCE and found in the palace archives of the Hittite capital, Boghazkoy, in northern Anatolia: Mitra is invoked to sanctify the treaty. A few centuries later, his name is found in the Rig Veda, where he is invoked as a deity of order and justice. In India, the name Mitra may be translated as "treaty." Mitra's role as divine mediator and dispenser of justice was thus established well before the Romans assimilated this Indo-Persian deity into their own ever-expanding pantheon.

In the Zoroastrian sacred text known as the Avesta, Mithras is described as the genius of both diurnal and nocturnal celestial light. Referred to as the "Lord of Wide Pastures," he bestows beauty and fertility upon Earth, and defends worshippers of Ahura Mazda against the devas, considered malevolent by Zoroastrians. Mithras is all-seeing, all knowing, and forever just.

Tarsus, the capital of Cilicia, was the home of a cult dedicated to Perseus, slayer of Medusa, who is frequently portrayed wearing a distinctive Phrygian cap, similar to that worn by Mithras in his Roman temples. According to Herodotus, the Persians – the Zoroastrian people who worshipped Mithras and wrote hymns extolling him – derive their name from Perses, the son of Perseus.

The Bull-Slayer and the Invincible Sun

The central icon of Rome's Mithras cult was the tauroctony or bull-slaying scene. Depictions of Mithras, caped and wearing his trademark Phrygian cap, were found deep inside his temples – cave-like structures known as mithraea. (Mithraea were sometimes built within natural caverns.) Kneeling upon a bull's back and with one leg extended, Mithras plunges a knife or short sword into the bull's neck, simultaneously pulling the face of the beast skyward, usually by the nose. Sometimes, sheaves of wheat emerge from the bull's wound or its tail.

Other players are also often included in this scene: a dog and a snake lap at the blood or wheat that issues from the wound. A bowl typically appears in the foreground, while a scorpion is regularly found clutching the bull's genitals with its claws, and a raven watches from above. Also typically featured are twin torch-bearers, named Cautes and Cautopates, who stand respectively on either side of the scene. Cautes points his torch upward, while Cautopates points his towards Earth. Anthropomorphic representations of the sun (Sol/Helios) and moon (Luna/Selene) driving their chariots through the sky are often found behind this bull-slaying scene, which is consistently rendered in a very pious and reverent manner.

Over time, Mithras became associated with the Roman imperial solar cult, established by Aurelian in 274 CE. The epithet *Sol Invictus* ("the unconquerable sun") was frequently attached to his name. From its beginnings among the tribes of the Near East, to its inclusion in the cult of the Roman Emperor himself, the religion of Mithras astounds and bewilders historians to this day, who seek to delve deeply into its secret rites.

– ANTHONY TETH

More information on Mithras is available at http://TheWitchesAlmanac.com /AlmanacExtras/.

the fixed stars

Spica

The Fortunate One

23 Degrees of Libra

WHILE THE PLANETS twirl quickly, encircling the Sun in a stately dance, the fixed stars drift ever so slowly across the sphere of space that comprises our zodiac. Because the stars appeared to be stationary, relative to each other and to the Earth, they were grouped in symbolic patterns called constellations. The fixed stars require over 72 years to move across a single degree of the zodiac. They have been important to astrologers since earliest times. The term "fixed stars" developed as a way to distinguish the distant stars from the more rapidly moving planets.

Contemporary astrologers know that these distant stars have a real pulsating life force all their own. The fixed stars – members of distant galaxies that slowly rotate and expand – are linked to a vast store of important information. Their messages are rather like footnotes, adding to the interpretation of the closer planetary cycles. Some fixed stars are benevolent, while others are considered sinister. Whether they impact the horoscope of an individual or are prominent in worldwide astrology trends, the fixed stars offer significant insights. They clarify and add valuable details to all predictions and forecasts. Fixed stars are said to "cast no rays," which means that the only aspect they can make is a close conjunction, with an orb of three degrees or less, to a passing planet or luminary.

260 light-years distant from Earth are two jolly and joyful blue giant stars orbiting each other so that they appear to move as one. Together these binary stars are called Spica. They present an eternal theme of friendship and support, the perfect partnership. Located at the 23rd degree of Libra

in the familiar tropical zodiac, Spica champions the best of justice and true, loyal companionship.

The great classical astrologer Hipparchus is thought to have used data provided by Spica to establish the precession of the equinoxes and to develop the pattern of great world ages. About 3200 BCE in Egypt, a temple to the Goddess Menat (also called Hathor) was built and oriented toward Spica. Ptolemy catalogued Spica as having a nature of Mercury combined with Venus and Jupiter. Nicholas Copernicus depended on Spica for his research on the precession of the equinoxes. The Elizabethan astrologer William Lilly referred to the significance of Spica and other fixed stars in his book *Christian Astrology*. The star featured on the flag of the Brazilian state Pará is Spica. The heroes of Alastair Reynolds' science fiction novel, *Pushing Ice*, are carried to Spica by aliens. Spica appears in the video game Ar Tonelico as the name of one of the characters. The god Apollo instructed a crow or raven to follow Spica's light in order to collect sacred water from the celestial cup in the sky (aka the Big Dipper). On a clear night, stargazers can still trace the bird's flight by locating the bright star Arcturus in the Dipper's handle and then following the arc of distance forward to see Spica. Astronomy students remember this technique by saying "follow the arc to Arcturus and speed on to Spica."

Spica's name comes from a Latin term meaning ear of grain. It is one of only fifteen Behenian stars. Behenian is an Arabic word meaning *root*. The Behenian stars are revered for their ritual magic applications. Talismans are constructed to magically harness their powers. The Sun, Moon, a planet, or the ascendant within three degrees of a Behenian star is thought to be profoundly impacted by these magical properties.

Astrologers have always considered Spica, often called "the fortunate one," to be among the most benevolent stars. This lucky star assures wealth, fame, and glamour. Currently located at about 23 degrees of Libra, Spica provides a cool oasis of comfort in the turbulent *Via Combusta* of the zodiac. The *Via Combusta*, or explosive road, spans 15 degrees of Libra to 15 degrees of Scorpio. It is highlighted by a variety of sinister and malevolent stars that can have a debilitating impact on astrological placements in that area, depending upon other factors in the horoscope.

During the coming year, the planet Saturn will transit Spica. Since Saturn is exalted in the sign of Libra, its close proximity to Spica should have a profound impact. From May 17 – August 3, 2012, Saturn will hover within a degree of Spica. Matters related to health, real estate, partnerships, and justice can improve. Practical work with friends as well as metaphysical studies are likely to be in a positive phase at this time. From August 8 – 18, 2012, Mars will join Saturn near Spica in Libra, adding intensity to this pattern. In world affairs, important legal and political matters can be emphasized. The Libra New Moon on October 15, 2012 will almost exactly conjoin Spica. Lifestyle improvements affecting many can be unfolding. Watch for celebrity marriage news and landmark decisions in the courts during the four weeks following the New Moon in October.

Those born October 13 – 19 of any year will have the Sun in conjunction with Spica. This enhances spiritual interests, opportunities for advancement, and brings an aura of dignity and respect. Astrological placements from 20 – 26 degrees of Libra will be influenced by this benevolent star. Check your own horoscope to see if Spica impacts you.

Keynotes for Spica in the Birth Chart

With the Sun: Happiness, helpful relatives, status, and financial security.

With the Moon: Advanced technology, inventions, and family wealth can provide opportunities. There are exceptionally nice residences.

With Mercury: Cleverness makes problem solving a breeze. There is eloquence and linguistic skill.

With Venus: Wonderful friendships and social success; artistic ability is present.

With Mars: Good judgment, a quick mind, and talent in the martial arts or yoga can be present.

With Jupiter: Good fortune with investments, academic honors.

With Saturn: Popular with many friends of all age groups; beneficial charitable acts.

With Uranus: Enjoyable business opportunities, freedom, good networking skills.

With Neptune: Good family heritage, gain through a legacy or investment, talent in witchcraft as well as music, dance, or the fine arts.

With Pluto: There is strategic ability to influence associates and draw loyal supporters.

With the Part of Fortune: Beauty is a part of the surroundings; there is an excellent standard of living.

With the Ascendant: Honor and advancement come easily. Stellar opportunities and good connections assure happiness.

Note: Arista, Azimech, and Alarph are all less commonly used names for Spica. They derive from Arabic root words and have been translated as "the undefended" and "grape gatherer."

– DIKKI-JO MULLEN

Winter came down to our home one night quietly pirouetting in on silvery-toed slippers of snow, And we, we were children once again.
— BILL MORGAN, JR.

SPRING

MARCH 2012. The month represents a dynamic transition from winter to spring across the country as the sun's rays shine more directly, warming the Earth. Lingering cold air at high latitudes and elevations creates a dynamic contrast that can spawn powerful storms on occasion. The effects of these storms have regional and local differences. A few storms bring heavy rain, muggy air and an occasional thunderstorm to the deep south. Farther north, heavy snow occurs several times this month from New England to the Great Lakes. Recent trends bringing deep snow to the mountainous west are likely to continue and travelers in California should remain alert to the possibility of mudslides. Very dry conditions are likely in Florida.

APRIL 2012. The sun's warmth brings the normal high temperature beyond 80 degrees to cities such as Miami, Phoenix and Houston. This is accompanied by an increase in thunderstorms and other severe weather activity in the Gulf States and southern Great Plains. Where ocean waters are slow to warm,

long spells of cool and damp weather persist. New England and the Pacific Northwest are especially prone to fleeting sunshine and cool temperatures. Travelers to Boston and Seattle can expect temperatures in the 50s with spells of drizzle. Heavy wet snow can fall in the mountains and a late season blizzard blankets the Northern Plains and briefly paralyzes Minneapolis.

MAY 2012. The peak of the tornado season arrives in May, with the greatest risk existing from the Southern Plains to the Ohio Valley; the so called "Tornado Alley". It is notable that there are other smaller areas away from that region that also have a disproportionate number of nature's most violent storms. Southwest New York and Connecticut, along with western Massachusetts connect and form a zone prone to damaging tornadoes. Similar conditions exist in southeast North Carolina, as well as central Florida. Tornadoes are much less frequent in the West, though occasional tornadoes have been spotted in Central California, western Washington State and Montana. Late spring should not be as severe along the Mississippi River this year.

SUMMER

JUNE 2012. In the Northern hemisphere, the sun reaches its highest zenith during the summer solstice. Still, the warmest temperatures are a month or so later on average. This occurs as the planet releases the sun's warming rays with a longer wavelength; thus, a longer process. The uneven nature of planetary heating defines our weather and long term climate. During the summer, temperatures are relatively even and moisture is abundant. Thunderstorms can occur in most places where rainfall can be heavy. Winds are strong near such systems. Elsewhere, temperatures are hot away from cooling sea breezes. Ocean waters warm: a preface to the pending hurricane season. Three days of 90' weather brings heat-wave conditions to many eastern cities, while the West is generally warm and dry. An isolated tornado may whirl in New England, the Great Lake states and the Northern Plains.

JULY 2012. Summer sizzles this month, as thermometers record temperatures routinely above 100 degrees in the Southwest and occasionally from Texas to the Canadian border. In these places, air is arid and the risk of fires runs high. West Coast temperatures vary greatly. The cool Humboldt ocean current and attending ocean breezes keeps the shoreline comfortably cool, while, just a few miles inland, readings reach the century mark. Hot and humid weather is prevalent throughout the East, with an occasional incursion of cool air triggering brief but memorable thunderstorms in the Northeast. Squally winds can attend such storms, which weaken upon reaching the ocean front. On Cape Cod, Long Island, and along coastal Maine, low clouds and fog persist each day until mid-morning, with a few hours of 80 degree warmth in the afternoons. A brief tropical storm brews in the Caribbean, which brings flooding rains to Central America.

AUGUST 2012. Tropical storms and hurricanes are generated and sustained by water temperatures of 80 degrees or greater in both the Atlantic basin and Pacific Ocean. Hurricanes south of California form first. Though they rarely affect the United States directly, they carry moisture north through the intermountain West, creating monsoon season there. In the Atlantic, the frequency of hurricanes increases rapidly through the month, beginning in the western Atlantic, before being generated off the coast of Africa by the end of the month. Rainfall is heaviest though the Appalachians from Georgia to Maine. A hurricane threatens landfall in Florida before crossing into the Gulf of Mexico. The nation's heartland enjoys generally warm and dry weather.

AUTUMN

SEPTEMBER 2012. Even as the sun is three months past its greatest output in the northern hemisphere, tropical water temperatures are at their peak and well beyond 80 degrees in the tropical Atlantic. The height of the hurricane season has arrived with the greatest occurrence of these storms from the 10th to the 15th of the month. Generally, about one hurricane makes landfall in the United States, though fewer storms have directly affected the United States in recent years. Longer term averages are likely to resume, with the East Coast and Florida especially prone. It is notable that New England is particularly vulnerable after escaping a serious land-falling hurricane for several decades. Elsewhere, the dry season has arrived through much of the country, as cool evenings arrive across the North. The fire season arrives in the West, especially in California and Nevada.

OCTOBER 2012. The threat from the most dangerous hurricanes eases somewhat in October as any storm weakens somewhat while approaching the Gulf Coast. Fading sun light brings a change of season and bright foliage, first near the Canadian border by the 10th and then from the southern Appalachians to Colorado's Aspens by the 25th. In general, conditions are dry nationwide, though mountain rains are a daily event in the Rockies and elsewhere in the mountainous west. Fires sweep through the canyon lands of southern California, though not as extensively as in recent years. An early frost ends the growing season in the Central Plains and Montana.

NOVEMBER 2012. Dry and chilly weather settles through the Northeast and much of the country. The hurricane season effectively ends as activity is limited to a small area near Central America. Several weak disturbances accompany advancing cold air from the Great Lakes to the Rockies and a thin snow cover can appear in a few areas. Cool breezes blow through Florida, with sweater weather arriving in Orlando and Tampa by Thanksgiving. Key West receives squally rains from a tropical wave of low pressure. In California, the risk for fire remains high in the south, even as the season's first Pacific storms bring cooling rains from San Francisco to Seattle. Meaningful snowfalls blanket the Cascades and northern Rockies, while the average high temperature in Phoenix drops to about 85 degrees.

AUTUMN

DECEMBER 2012. Winter weather slowly deepens across the country, with the greatest chances for snowfall early in the month in western New York state, the Rockies and California's Sierra Nevada. Cold air is limited for a while in New England and Mid Atlantic region with a lack of snow cover. However, chances for a White Christmas are higher than normal in cities such as New York and Boston. The Southeast is generally cool and dry and the risk for an early freeze exists in Northern Florida. The central and southern plains are milder than normal and an abundant winter wheat crop is likely in Texas and elsewhere. Central and southern California rainfall increases somewhat, though winds remain gusty with an elevated fire risk.

JANUARY 2013. Not only is the sun at its weakest influence in January, but the white color of an increasing snow cover through much of the nation reflects incoming solar radiation back into space. This leads to chilly days and frigid nights, with sub-freezing temperatures as far south as the Gulf Coast. The air is so cold that little moisture is available to produce wide-scale snow and rain, except across the West Coast, where windswept gales persist, spawned by Pacific-born storms. A glancing blow from an ocean storm also clips the outer banks of North Carolina and Cape with brief blizzard conditions. Lake effect snows are heavy in Buffalo and the eastern suburbs of Cleveland. In the Northern Plains, the Mercury plummets to 30 below zero in Minneapolis and nearly as cold in Chicago. The severe cold eases late in the month with a brief January thaw for most.

FEBRUARY 2013. The pace of storm formation and intensity quickens in February and as many as four East Coast storms threaten the region. Snow can fall on all major cities there, with above normal snow fall from Washington to Boston. Coastal gales will threaten local shorelines with flooding. The West Coast will also be stormy with snow falling in the mountains and heavy rain bringing mudslides to hilly terrain near San Francisco and as far south as San Diego. Even Phoenix enjoys some winter rains accompanied by cooler air. Flagstaff receives heavy snowfall and travel is limited through the intermountain west. Cold and dry weather is likely across the Midwest with snowfall limited to the Great Lake shoreline.

Sitting at the Crossroads

THE Yoruba of southwestern Nigeria have long honored a pantheon of deities known as Orisa who are the emanations of the high God Olodumare. Among the many deities are the primordial Orisa known as Irunmole. One of the primordial deities is the ubiquitous Esu who embodies the principle of potential in the universe. His presence is so pervasive it is said that no one can truly list all of his names and attributes. He is the single Orisa who remains outside a complete understanding or categorization. While Esu has many roles, his actions as the divine gatekeeper, messenger, enforcer, trickster and the conveyer of sacrifices are most prominent.

Because Esu represents all possibilities, he is very often seen as an ambiguous being. Unlike the other Orisa, he can be represented as male or female, young or old in iconography. When depicted as a male, very often his hair is styled in a single braid down the center of his head which is a female fashion. When portrayed as a female, the hair is fashioned in a braid that mirrors a barely disguised phallus. Another example of contradiction are the depictions of Esu sucking his thumb versus smoking a pipe. The former example points to his youth, the latter his old age. All of these ambiguities emphasize his ability to be all possibilities at once and a true agent of change.

Also figuring prominently in his shrines is the phallus. While this can be construed as representing fertility and masculine energy, it is more indicative of his willful nature. Just as one could say that the penis has a mind of its own, so does Esu; defying all sense of boundaries and willful with a sense of order that is his own. The central role of the phallus as one of his symbols illustrates his ability to penetrate all barriers.

Gatekeeper of the Yoruba Pantheon

Esu's ability to assume any guise and to penetrate all worlds makes it easy to understand why he is the gatekeeper in the Yoruba pantheon. He is said to live at the center of all crossroads — all points of convergence. As we approach the many crossroads in our lives, he can either help us onto the path that brings things together or the path that tears things asunder. The crossroads is certainly an apropos place to encounter the deity of potential. The choices are manifold. His is the ability to open all doors

Esu is the gatekeeper. Thus it is with him that all must begin and all must end. Because of this, all ritual actions of the Yoruba must begin and end with Esu. At the onset of any ritual, the rite is opened with a prayer to Esu. The body of the ritual follows. Then, the ritual is closed with a prayer for Esu to bring the actions of the ritual into manifestation. Because Esu is all potential and also because of his capricious nature, ending without proper prayer to Esu could result in possibilities other than the one desired.

Sacred Rhythms of the Orisa

A form of worship commonly practiced in Yoruba communities is a drumming. In these meetings, drummers will come together to beat out the sacred rhythms of the Orisa, while a trained singer will lead all in a call and response type of singing. At the same time, believers will fill the central area in front of the drums, dancing sacred steps that along with their voices invoke the presence of the deities in the bodies of their priests via possession.

Again, the first to be sung and danced for will be Esu. As the drums beat out his sacred rhythm, one can often see a divine possession begin to take place as one of his priests begins to dance with one foot flat and pounding the floor in front, and the other foot on tiptoe. This peculiar dance which almost looks like a limp is indicative of Esu having one foot in each of the worlds – the world of deities and the world of men. Often a priest's hand will go to his forehead, index finger pointing up, mimicking the phallic braid seen in his iconography.

The drummers will incite Esu to take possession of his priest, if this does not happen, they will move on to another Orisa. In the end the drummers will close the rite by again returning to the sacred rhythms of Esu.

Messenger and Enforcer

All beings below Olodumare are subject to the web of destiny; including the Orisa. Esu is the gatekeeper and also the enforcer, overseeing the interactions between Olodumare and the Orisa as well as interactions between the Orisa and humans. As such, he is the policeman of both divinity and humanity, reporting the actions of both back to Olodumare. In the case of the divinities, he is charged with enforcing their correctness of action and that they heed the divinations they receive and that they make appropriate corrective offerings. In the case of mankind, he is charged with oversight on the correctness and timeliness of the worship, offerings to the divinities and compliance with advice given during divination. Failure in any of these cases will result in opening the door that leads to chaos.

Interpreter of Fate

As the enforcer of the Olodumare and the Orisa, Esu is intimately linked with the various divination systems of the Yoruba. He is especially linked with the supreme system known as Ifa which is ruled by Orunmila, the Orisa of Knowledge. These two Orisa are particularly linked because of their respective roles in the divine pantheon. As the enforcer, it is up to Esu to inspect the correctness of worship and sacrifice and as the interpreter of fate, it is Orunmila who prescribes means (sacrifice and ritual) that put one back on track with destiny.

Esu forces order via the disorder that he creates. His turmoil will stimulate many to visit the diviner priests to solve a situation. Esu watches the divination process – his face in carved into the divining tray, facing the diviner. In the end, when Ifa directs an individual to make offering to a particular deity, it is Esu who delivers the offering to the deity.

Stirring the Pot

Besides being the enforcer, Esu is also the trickster creating chaos and tribulation that brings about change. While this is often a bitter way to learn a lesson, it ultimately does lead to a nexus of learning. A good example is the following story:

There came to pass a day when two friends were working in their adjoining plots of land. A man came down the road between them on horseback. Both of them noticed the fine hat the man was wearing. When they broke for lunch they each commented on the wonderful hat. The first said that he had never seen such a fine white hat. The other remarked that it was indeed the finest he had ever seen; however, he insisted it was black. The discussion got very heated and led to blows. Each vowed to kill the other for insinuating that he was a liar. Just then, Esu, who had disguised himself earlier as the horseman, came again on his horse and asked what the fight was about. After each had given their version of the story, Esu showed them the hat that he had worn, which was white on the right side and black on the left. He announced that they were both correct, but each had a different perspective. Revealing himself to them as Esu, he verbally chastised them for making foolish vows.

When we are stuck in the inertia of life, Esu stirs the pot of chaos and creates new possibilities. He employs change, turmoil and sacrifice as vehicles for new opportunities that allow us to return to our destinies. In this case true friends need to consider the other's perspective or suffer the loss of friendship. Via turmoil and havoc Esu reminds men that they are friends for a reason. Further they should be wary of making foolish vows. Esu's presence is necessary in all situations where boundaries are crossed, decisions must be made, or where people communicate with each other or with the other world.

Shrines and Offerings

Like all Orisa, Esu's shrine is very particular. In Yorubaland his most sacred object is a piece of laterite stone inserted either into the ground or into a special pot that has herbs and earth in it. Laterite used for an Esu shrine is called *yangi*. At times his symbols will be covered with an overturned pot that has a hole through it. This enables the uninitiated to make offerings without profaning his image by looking upon it. Dance rods used for special occasions that are effigies of the Orisa are hung around his altar upside down, to symbolize his trickster nature.

In African Diaspora traditions, his shrine is made of cement into which special herbs and objects are placed. The front of the molded head is embellished with facial features made of cowries. In keeping with his identity as gatekeeper, he is usually placed in a cabinet close to the front door of the home.

A typical offering made to Esu by both initiates and non-initiates in African Diaspora traditions is to fill three small brown paper bags with different kinds of sweets and 21 pennies each. (Do not use pepper or spearmint sweets.) Cleanse yourself with each bag by passing it over your entire body. Leave one bag at three different crossroads. At each location, direct a prayer to Esu asking for the changes that you would like to manifest. Be careful what you ask for, you just may get it.

– IFADOYIN SANGOMUYIWA
Nigerian Priest to Sango and Babalawo, Father of Secrets

Strengthening the above offering would be the prayer that is used in Yorubaland:

Esù òkiri òkò
Esù ota Òrìsà
Olágbokùn
Alágbárá
Omokùnrin dúdú ìta
Bàbá kékeré
Esù Òdàrà omokùnrin ìdelofin
E lé sónsó s'órí ese elése
Kò je kò sì je kì eni je gbe mì
E fi òkútà dípò iyo
E túká má se é sà
Erejà
'Lásúnkàn'
Esù olá ìlú
Eni se ebo ní oore ni Esù ngbè
Òbembe níjó
Lágemo orun
A kìí l'ówó lâi mú ti Esù kúrò
A kìí l'áyo lâi mú ti Esù kúrò
A kìí se ohun rere lâi mú ti Esù kúrò
Esù, mo júbà o
Esù, má se mí
Eni ti kó se ebo
ni kí e se

Esù, bearer of stones. Esù, avenger of Òrìsà. Great fighter, Powerful one. Dark-skinned man of the outdoors. Small, revered man. Esù Odara from Ìdýlýfin. You sit down conspicuously on your victim's lap. You refuse to eat and likewise prevent your victims from peacefully enjoying their meal. You exchange salt for pebbles. You are difficult to reassemble once scattered. You collect dues from the marketplace. "Wealth-slides-near" Esù, the town's good fortune. It is the one who makes offerings who receives Esù's blessings. Great dancer, Indulgent child of heaven. We cannot enjoy wealth without giving Esù his due. We cannot be joyful without giving Esù his due. We cannot benefit from the good things in life without giving Esù his due. Esù, I pay homage to you. Esù, do not interfere negatively with my life. Esù, undo whosoever fails to make offering to you, appease you and respect you.

Anahita

Persian Mother of Waters

SHE IS THE Immaculate One, purity itself, our primal Zoroastrian goddess of waters. We can hardly encompass her complexity, but we begin with water. Anahita is associated with lakes, rivers and seas. She is "wide flowing," assuming vast tasks of fertility: "the life-increasing, the herd-increasing, the flock-increasing one who makes prosperity for all countries." The deity also presides over green things, especially healing plants and crops, encouraging tender shoots to greet the world. Anahita also exerts fertility magic for women in an intimate way, purifying birth waters and aiding the flow of milk to nourish newborns. Beyond her earthy powers, metaphors nudge us – water has been identified with wisdom since ancient times.

As below, so above. Sometimes we see the deity depicted with wings, cosmological ruler of stars and planets. In a Sufi poem, Anahita rides a chariot driven by four weather horses, Wind, Rain, Clouds and Sleet. Zoroastrians believe that the ancient goddess is a deification of the planet Venus itself. Alternatively, she may stand in "statuesque stillness, ever observed," shouldering a water pitcher and attended by her sacred birds, the dove and the peacock.

Agleam in gold

The supreme goddess is tall, strong, and beautiful. The Persians love to bedeck her in gold. Anahita wears a tiara of stars and shines with gold earrings, breastplate, necklace, bracelets, kerchief and ankle-high boots laced with gold. She wraps herself in a cloak embroidered with gold and hung with thirty otter skins.

The Anahita cult believes that this Great Lady, the daughter of Ahura

Mazda, and wife of Mithra, should dwell in stately places. Her temples glitter with gold, silver, and marble as well as fragrant wood. Veneration rose to fever pitch during the fourth-century reign of King Artaxerxes II, a devotee. Anahita's sanctuary at Ecbatana was among the glories of the ancient world. The palace encompassed four-fifths of a mile, its edifice cedar and cypress, the wood plated with gold or sometimes silver. Every floor tile was silver. Gold and silver bricks covered the vast exterior, dazzling the eye, shimmering like a mirage in the Persian sun.

This palace served a dual purpose for the king. Plutarch, ever gossipy, tells us that Artaxerxes installed his concubine Aspasia as priestess at Ecbatana "that she might spend the rest of her days in strict chastity." We have no contemporary account of the lives of other priestesses. Perhaps they were celibate or perhaps temple prostitutes, similar to earlier Ishtar celebrants. Some historians believe that the temple was destroyed in 324 BCE by Alexander the Great because Anahita neglected to heal his lover and companion Hephaestion, who died in Ecbatana.

In her honor

The goddess appears as the female creative principle beside all-powerful Ahura Mazda, aiding his work of Creation. As a later cult figure, Anahita teaches the prophet Zarathustra how to prevail for justice among mortals and how to perform sacrifices. She, herself, particularly welcomes white heifers and green branches. The sacrament may be accompanied by prayers for knowledge and insight, followed by an offering of water. She is bountiful to those who please her, harsh to those who do not, and effective against evil spirits. Worship by praise may ramp up effectiveness, for deities enjoy sweet talk as much as lovers. Adherents ritually address her as "Great Lady Anahita, glory and life-giver of our nation, mother of sobriety and benefactor of humanity."

– Barbara Stacy

Bottle Trees

Inspiration for the Ecologically-Minded Witch

ALTHOUGH THEY sparkle just as beautifully in the sunlight as the most expensive stained glass, only a few years ago bottle trees were dismissed as eccentric anomalies, occasionally observed tucked away along dusty byways in the rural South and brightening the gardens of the very poor. Today, with recycled items featured in the creation of all sorts of outdoor patio ornaments, the status of the bottle tree has changed. Now admired show pieces, bottle trees are spotted among the fancy formal beds of London's prestigious Chelsea Flower Show. A bottle tree delights visitors at Walt Disney World's Epcot Center. Bottle trees are showcased by proud landscape designers from Michigan to the Pacific Northwest, New England to Europe, and from South America to Africa. Entrepreneurs even offer them for sale on-line.

A bottle tree is simply discarded empty bottles slid onto bare tree limbs. A dead or stripped-down tree with branches can be the canvas for really beautiful creations. Variations exist: a Florida gardener fashioned one by placing bottles among the fronds of a palm tree. Large nails atop fence posts can substitute for a tree as can an upended pitch fork with the handle partially buried, so that the tines can hold small bottles.

Glass Prisons and Magic Lamps

Archaeologists have determined that, by the ninth century CE, bottle trees were popular in many parts of Europe, Asia, and Africa. There is speculation that they are far more ancient. Glass was first invented about 3000 BCE in Africa. By 1600 BCE, hollow bottles were common in Egypt and Mesopotamia. For generations, magical folklore has maintained that bottles and spheres of glass can lure and trap wayward spirits, thus averting evil spells. Tales of imps in glass prisons and of geniis trapped in lamps that date back at least one-thousand years to Arabia and the Sahara probably contributed to the origin of modern bottle trees. Europeans created witch balls – hollow globes of colored glass with a hole in the bottom – to detain questionable energies.

At sunrise, these night crawlers are destroyed by the bright light and their shadows and ill intentions are bottled away for good.

From Trash to Treasure

The bottle tree tradition offers an inexpensive inspiration for the eco-logically-minded witch to try some imaginative recycling. The glorious jewel tones which appear when the glass is touched by sunshine offer appealing highlights for Mother Earth. With a little patient collecting, yoga enthusiasts might assemble a bottle tree in the chakra colors for meditation. Traditionally, teal or turquoise glass is the best choice if negative entities, or threatening hexes or ghosts are suspected. A tree covered in bright emerald green bottles can be dedicated as a prosperity charm. The array of cast-off bottles available suggests numerous other possibilities.

A Kaleidoscope of Colors

A haphazard kaleidoscope of multi-colored bottles is the current most popular style. A gardener in the Lone Star State has honored the blue bonnet, the state flower of Texas, with a bottle tree fashioned of blue bottles atop layers of green glass. Another pretty idea is an entire tree covered in alternating clear and green bottles. When touched by the Sun, this resembles Yuletide twinkle-lights. Bright royal blue bottles are often the most coveted. Perhaps that's because blue glass radiates the healing and peaceful mood which is so welcomed in today's stressful world.

Mix a weak solution of ammonia and detergent and add it to a tub of hot water. Wash some cast off wine, beer, olive oil, or milk of magnesia bottles until they gleam. Now you are prepared to discover their beauty and harness their magical potentials by creating a bottle tree for your very own garden or covenstead.

– ELAINE NEUMEIER

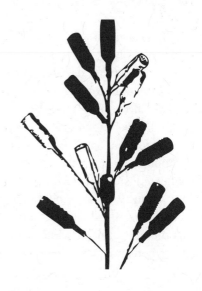

Astrology of the Vampires

Count Saint Germain's System of Birthday Years

THERE IS A provocative consistency to the many eye-witness reports attesting that the character known as the Count Saint Germain has remained alive for centuries. An alluring, sympathetic, kind and charming figure, he changes the lives of all who encounter him. The Count Saint Germain may be recognized by his elegant dress and courtly manners, his talent as a violinist and, not least, by his signature glowing red ruby, worn either as a ring or as a tie pin.

The fabulous Saint Germain has been spotted in Greece, France, Germany, Italy, Russia and New Orleans. His true identity is mysterious and has long been subject for debate and speculation. One tradition suggests that he is really Christopher Columbus who, instead of perishing in disgrace, as history records, actually escaped alive. The Count's living presence has been documented since at least the seventeenth century. The Count's supernaturally long life has been attributed to his diet of oatmeal, white wine and chicken consumed in small portions.

Legend whispers that this diet is a cover for Saint Germain's practice of vampirism.

Schooled in mysticism and the arts and sciences, Saint Germain speaks eleven languages. He even created a whole system of astrology. The gist of it is simple, yet it provides a helpful guide to planning each year of life for optimum success. The Count's path to eternally renew and rebirth each year is based on linking the years of one's life to the twelve houses of the horoscope.

If you are familiar with your own birth chart, take a look at it. Incorporate the meanings of the sign ruling the cusp and any planets there into the whole picture. For those unfamiliar with astrology, just look at the keywords for each house and use those as a focus for your activities this year. You will be amazed at how this helps you to live in tune with the cosmic rhythms. What happens if, like the legendary Count, you pass age 100? Well, just start the pattern over again!... And continue for each new century...

– DIKKI-JO MULLEN

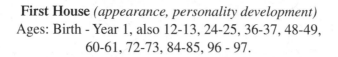

First House *(appearance, personality development)*
Ages: Birth - Year 1, also 12-13, 24-25, 36-37, 48-49,
60-61, 72-73, 84-85, 96 - 97.

Second House *(earning ability, cash assets, material possessions)*
Ages: 11-12, 23-24, 35-36, 47-48, 59-60, 71-72, 83-84, 95 -96.

Third House *(neighbors and siblings, transportation, communication skills)*
Ages: 10-11, 22-23, 34-35, 46-47, 58-59, 70-71, 82-83, 95-96.

Fourth House *(parents, residences, investment,
real estate, end of life circumstances, subconscious)*
Ages: 9-10, 21-22, 33-34, 45-46, 57-58, 69-70, 81-82, 93-94.

Fifth House *(creative gifts, romance, hobbies, children)*
Ages: 8-9, 20-21, 32-33, 44-45, 56-57, 68-69, 80-81, 92-93.

Sixth House *(health, pets, employees, daily work, aunts and uncles)*
Ages: 7-8, 19-20, 31-32, 43-44,55-56, 67-68, 79-80, 91-92.

Seventh House *(partnerships, marriage, legalities, ethics, opposition)*
Ages: 6-7, 18-19, 30-31, 42-43, 54-55, 66-67, 78-79, 90-91.

Eighth House *(invested and inherited assets,
taxes, insurance, death, reincarnation, spirit world)*
Ages: 5-6, 17-18, 29-30, 41-42, 53-54, 65-66, 77-78, 89-90.

Ninth House *(religion and philosophy, higher education,
foreign travel, in-laws, grandchild-grandparent interactions)*
Ages: 4-5, 16-17, 28-29, 40-41, 52-53, 64-65, 76-77, 88-89.

Tenth House *(fame, recognition, career)*
Ages: 3-4, 15-16, 27-28, 39-40, 51-52, 63-64, 75-76, 87-88, 99- 100.

Eleventh House *(goals, friendships, government and humanitarian interests)*
Ages: 2-3, 14-15, 26-27, 38-39, 50-51, 62-63, 74-75, 86-87, 98-99.

Twelfth House *(solitude, wilderness,
self-created problems, confinement, large animals, unknown enemies)*
Ages: 1-2, 13-14, 25-26, 37-38, 49-50, 61-62, 73-74, 85-86, 97-98.

The Frog

"May it please the frogs, during the many rains that sustain our cattle in their hundreds, to prolong our life!"
– Frog Hymn, *Rig Veda 7.103*

A FOAMY NEST floats in the calm, primal waters of prehistory, nurturing hundreds of eggs to hatching. New lives venture out, nibbling on algae, and stretching their developing hind legs. Their front legs emerge, while their tails diminish. Trading gills for lungs, they have matured.

A frog's life cycle echoes the cycle of life. Beginning in Earth's primordial waters, the frog then transforms to enable it to live on land. Amphibian, or "two-natured," is a title earned by the frog's ability to traverse with ease between water and dry land. Ancient Egyptians used the frog hieroglyph to mean "repeating life."

The frog's changing nature does not end with maturity. Each year of their long lives, they hibernate during the dry or winter season. At that time, their systems slow to the point of appearing dead. During hibernation, frogs become severely dehydrated. In cold climates, they even freeze, forming ice crystals that cut through their cell walls, stopping blood flow. And yet, with the spring, frogs thaw and return. Resurrection! That's something to sing about.

The Nile Chorus

Frog choruses have announced the coming rain and rising waters of the Nile for millennia. Frogs symbolize fertility, good fortune, resurrection and rebirth – with the exception of one bad plague recounted in the Bible's *Book of Exodus*. Still, early Christians adopted cross-adorned frogs to symbolize resurrection on Judgment Day.

Egypt's four male primordial gods are depicted with frog heads (their female counterparts have serpent heads). Considering the frog's longevity and tenacity for survival, their capacity to bounce back from injuries, and talent at procreating, what better symbol is there of life's essence?

Heqet, Frog Goddess of Birth, Death, and Life

The Egyptian frog goddess, Heqet, represents the cult of the dead and eternal life. As goddess of water, birth and resurrection, she breathes life into human bodies after the ram god, Khnum forms them on his potter's wheel. Heqet's priestesses may have served as midwives, while pregnant women donned frog amulets, so as to receive the goddess' protection during childbirth.

Frog amulets were also buried with the dead: those in special favor were given their own mummified frogs to guide them to the underworld and back. Heqet is chronicled resting at the feet of Osiris' funeral bier. Later, she breathes life into Horus, who was conceived by Isis and the already-dead Osiris.

Frogs versus Toads

The difference between frogs and toads can be ambiguous – some languages don't even distinguish between the two species. It's not unusual for a frog characteristic to show up in a type of toad or vice versa. Generally, if it has long legs and webbed feet, it's a frog. A frog's body is similar to human proportions, while a toad has shorter limbs.

Frogs and toads possess very different reputations, however. Frogs are symbolic of life, heralds of spring rain, fertility, and fortune. A frog entering a house brings good luck, while a toad crossing your path is believed by many to bring misfortune. Toads were once thought to carry the souls of unborn children.

Sacred Frog Rites and Funerals

The Zhuang, the largest of China's ethnic minorities, venerate the frog. They believe the frog has great influence over his father, the thunder god. On the first day of the first month of the lunar year, Zhuang men hunt the hibernating frog. The first to find one is rewarded with good fortune. The frog is sacrificed, laid out in a precious coffin and paraded through town. Festivities conclude on the second day of the second lunar month, when the prior sacrificial frog-king's bones are exhumed and read for signs of the coming year's harvest. In Nepal, the Jyapu rice farmers honor the frogs in their fields on July's full moon. The rite, Byan Janakegu, means "feeding rice to the frogs."

There seems to be mythic agreement around the world that frogs' voices summon the rain. Most cultures also agree that the best instrument to mimic a frog's voice is the drum. Bronze rain drums were once the possessions of kings in Thailand. Among the Karen people, someone couldn't be wealthy without owning one. The drum's skin symbolizes a pond with rings radiating outward like ripples from a central sun. Bronze frogs adorn the rim, witnessing the essential combination of water and sun that brings a fertile harvest. The magical spirits of the frog drums convey wealth, status, and security. Often, they're buried with their owners.

Fairytale Frogs

All across Europe, frogs pop up in fairytales. In one version of *The Frog Prince*, a princess deceit-

fully agrees to allow a frog to become her companion, if he'll retrieve her golden ball from the well. Later during a fit of temper, she throws the frog against the wall, inadvertently lifting a shape-shifting curse from the frog, changing him back to a prince. Later versions of this story have the frog transformed by the princess' kiss. The frog is at ease crossing the boundaries between worlds and can guide people to do the same. In the Frog Prince, the patient frog guides the princess in her own transition from child to wife.

A frog plays a significant role in another Grimm's fairytale, *Sleeping Beauty* (also known as *Little Thorn Rose*). As the story begins, a childless couple's prayers are answered when, during the queen's bath, a frog emerges from the water and speaks to her. The frog predicts that the queen will conceive a daughter within the year – and she does. This frog demonstrates knowledge of the couple's fertility and perhaps can control it. Just as the frog can transition between water and land, so it guides the queen's transition into a new state of life: motherhood.

Sleeping Beauty – the story's long-awaited child – is later cursed by a spiteful wise woman, angered at not being invited to the baby shower. The curse initially dooms the baby princess to die, after pricking her finger on a spindle. Luckily, another kinder wise woman in attendance is able to mitigate this curse, changing the outcome to a profound, magical sleep. Spindles are a common motif in frog tales, signifying time's passage. This Pagan remnant warns us that, no matter what, death will someday claim us. It also promises that we will wake again from our long sleep.

Likewise, another fairytale princess, Snow White, whose life, in some versions of her tale, is also magically bestowed by a frog, falls into to a sleep so deep that she appears as dead as a hibernating frog. Her curse is broken in the same way as some variants of the story, *The Frog Prince* – with a kiss!

The Frog Hill Fest
On the surface, Asian frog festivals and European fairytales appear very different. Maybe before drawing that conclusion, however, we should consider the month of February, when Lupercalia was celebrated in Rome and another kind of madness occurs in the North. For three days in February, s-Hertogenbosch in the Netherlands changes its name to Oeteldonk, meaning "Frog Hill." Like Lupercalia, these three days are full of merriment and misrule. Conventions are turned on their heads during this Dutch festival, among the oldest celebrations of Carnival in the world.

Having been celebrated at least as far back as 1385, this spring festival features two ever-present characters: the Frog Prince and Knillis, the farmer. The festival begins with the Frog Prince arriving Sunday morning by train and heading to the marketplace.  There, a statue of Knillis is unveiled and will remain until the Frog Prince carts it away for "the burial" rite three days later.

Carnival in this "water-free swamp" is full of drink and song. One traditional tune proclaims "what fertile lands, realm plants with turnips and radishes and mounts of the cleanest sands." Yes, it's another agricultural festival celebrating the fertility of the land! Be assured, we aren't the first to note its similarities to the Festival of Osiris.

Leap Frog is another possible remnant of a fertility rite that survives today as both a game and a Morris Dance performed during Beltane (May Day). According to the Elder Faith of Ireland, the young men winning at leap frog could claim a kiss from their girl of choice. Nor is this love connection lost on Mother Goose who has her own rhyme, "the frog he would a-wooing go…"

Artemis of the Frogs

One title of the Greek moon goddess, Artemis, is Artemis Digaia Blaganitis, "Goddess of the Frogs." Her temples were in marshy, wet places where she received frogs as offerings. Leto, her mother, was forced to give birth to Artemis and her twin brother, Apollo, on Delos because it was a "floating island" unconnected to land – a description that brings a lily pad to mind.

Agrippa also attributed rulership of frogs to the moon. Agrippa's moon suffumigation recipe included a dried frog's head, bull's eyes, white poppy seeds, frankincense and camphor mixed with goose or menstrual blood. A frog's tongue was used in spells so as to benefit from the frog's reputation of singing in the manner of compelling the truth from someone. To be effective, a tongue from a still-living frog that was returned to the water was laid on the subject's breast.

Guardians of the Ankh of Life

Frogs don't actually breathe or drink. Instead they soak water and air through their skin. An old Italian healing remedy credits them with absorbing illness, too. For instance, placing a live frog in the patient's mouth absorbed thrush. Ponder that the next time someone complains of a frog in their throat!

Frogs truly are liminal beings. No wonder many cultures see a frog in the moon rather than a man. Like the moon, frogs are ever-transforming, ever-cycling and ever changing in form, size and even gender.

The frog's nature has proven long-lived and tenacious. They have a capacity to recover quickly from wounds and bear loads of offspring for the next generation. Frogs are described as wise and generous, while exhibiting a profound patience and willingness to excuse bad behavior in others. What better emblem could serve to guard the ankh of life?

– NIALLA NI MACHA

79

Sunshine Safety

Essential Oils and Photosensitization

WE'VE ALL HEARD the term aromatherapy – usually in connection with candles or bubble bath – but the true definition of aromatherapy is the use of essential oils for medicinal purposes. In fact, therapeutic use of essential oils is common in hospitals and burn centers throughout Europe.

Essential oils are produced from a diverse range of plant materials collected all over the world. Different parts of plants are steam distilled to create oils that are extremely concentrated. These oils are complex, containing anywhere from fifty to two hundred chemical constituents that interact with  our body systems to help strengthen and enhance our body's many functions. Some essential oils kill airborne microbes; others heal wounds; some reduce stress, or quell a cough. The list goes on.

However, some essential oils have properties that are not so desirable. Certain oils can cause adverse reactions when exposed to the sun. The term for this is photosensitization. Though these oils also possess beneficial qualities, they are not appropriate for every product or every application.

Risky Oils

One well-known group of essential oils notorious for causing photosensitization are the citrus oils. These are pressed from the peels of lemons, limes, bergamot etc.. Although harmless when not exposed to light, these oils should be avoided in products that might be used outdoors, such as lotions, powders, hair treatments and the like. It is ironic that the essential oils considered to be sunshine in a bottle should not be exposed to sunshine on your skin. There are exceptions to this. Grapefruit, sweet orange, grapefruit, and mandarin

are not photosensitizing agents. Since it can be difficult to remember which citrus oils are hazardous in the sun, many people simply avoid all citrus oils in sun products.

Citrus oils are not the only culprits that cause photosensitization, there are others. Here is a general list of essential oils that should not be used during exposure to the sun or tanning beds:

Angelica
Bergamot
Bitter Orange
Caraway
Cumin
Ginger
Lemon
Lemon Verbena
Lime
Lovage
Melissa

(Bear in mind new oils are being distilled regularly and research is limited.)

Seeking Treatment

Anyone can suffer any degree of photosensitivity. There are many variables including skin pigmentation, duration of exposure to the sun, and variety of essential oil used. Some reactions can take from twenty-four to forty-eight hours to surface.

If you suspect you are experiencing a photosensitive reaction the first thing to do is get out of the sun. You can try to remove the essential oil by "washing" the area with a non-essential oil like olive oil, almond oil or canola. This may be difficult if the essential oil has had time to penetrate the cells of the skin. Once sensitization has occurred the sun should be avoided for twenty-four hours. Skin should be protected until all signs of irritation subside.

The power of the sun has become more intense than ever with the accelerated depletion of the earth's ozone layer. Protecting our skin from the harmful effects of the sun's dangerous ultraviolet rays has become vitally important. A few simple ways to protect against the sun's ultraviolet radiation are to wear UV protective clothing, use a quality sunscreen, and abstain from applying essential oils that cause photosensitivity before playing outdoors or heading to the tanning booth.

– LINDA PATTERSON

Merry Meetings

*A candle in the window, a fire on the hearth,
a discourse over tea…*

This year *The Witches' Almanac* visits with author Judika Illes, whose books are devoted to spirituality, witchcraft, and the occult. Judika's books include *The Encyclopedia of 5000 Spells*; *The Encyclopedia of Spirits*; *The Encyclopedia of Mystics, Saints, and Sages*; *The Element Encyclopedia of Witchcraft*; *Pure Magic: A Complete Course in Spellcasting* and *The Weiser Field Guide to Witches*. She is also a certified aromatherapist, paraprofessional crisis counselor, public speaker, and an acclaimed card reader.

Judika, your books are considered an essential resource for those with an interest in witchcraft and the magical arts. What sort of life experiences or influences sparked your initial interest in these disciplines?

That's a question I'm constantly asked, but one that's actually very hard to answer. Why do any of us love whatever it is that we love? My interest in these topics was sparked extremely early. I fell in love with witches, witchcraft, divination, and the magical arts at an extremely young age and that passion remains unabated. It's difficult for me to say why. You could argue all sorts of reason – genetics, past life, destiny –

but whatever the reason, there it is. My earliest influences include the neighborhood in Queens where I grew up – I was transfixed by the storefront windows of local botanicas. I was fed a steady diet of fairytales, stimulating my devotion to Baba Yaga and Lilith. I was also a very precocious reader. I could read by the time I was three, and I was permitted to read anything I wanted. To this day, I'm a compulsive reader. Among the books lying around the house were books on astrology, tarot, and other forms of divination – I just consumed them.

What made you become a metaphysical writer?

Honestly, I never set out to be a metaphysical writer. That just happened; I fell into it. My original goal was to publish a book on traditional methods of enhancing fertility and healing infertility. I have a huge manuscript on these topics that remains unpublished. This derives from my own experiences back in the late 80s. The medical solutions suggested to me were unsatisfactory and so I began researching and eventually amassed a manuscript similar in size to the encyclopedias I have published. That was actually the first book I ever completed. A publisher saw the manuscript – there's a chapter on magic spells in it – and asked if I would write a more general book devoted to spellcraft, which eventually became the book now known as *Pure Magic*. I agreed in a minute – the magic arts are my first love.

Is it true that The Witches' Almanac *was instrumental in writing one of your books?*

That's right. After I completed *The Encyclopedia of 5000 Spells*, which was my third published work, I was asked by the publisher whether I would like to follow up with an encyclopedia of witchcraft. Initially, I was not overly enthusiastic – most encyclopedias of witchcraft, with very few exceptions, are not really about witches or their craft. Instead, they tend to be about witch hunting, written by outsiders to the Craft or they are focused on very narrow visions or definitions of witchcraft. I was a little resistant. But then I received a lovely note from someone representing the Non-Wiccan Witches Yahoo Group, thanking me for aspects of *5000 Spells*. They thanked me for making them feel represented. I entered into some correspondence and they were enthusiastic about my writing an encyclopedia

of witchcraft – one that would encompass a greater vision of witchcraft rather than a narrow one – and so I began to reconsider. I became more enthusiastic when I realized I could focus attention on those I considered to be the unsung heroes and heroines of witchcraft – especially Elizabeth Pepper, the founder and creative genius behind *The Witches' Almanac*. I thought she – as well as the *Almanac* – had been very overlooked, and I was grateful for the opportunity to shine a light upon her and it. In my determination to write about *The Witches' Almanac*, I met Elizabeth Pepper. I feel very grateful for this opportunity to communicate and correspond with her before she passed.

Who do you consider some other unsung heroes and heroines of witchcraft?

There are so many, but among those at the top of my list would be the author and publisher Paschal Beverly Randolph. Sybil Leek is hardly unsung but she has become very underappreciated.  All her books are currently out-of-print and she does not receive the credit that is due her. Marie Laveau is too often sensationalized and is not given the serious credit that she deserves – she is a tremendous influence on modern Western magical and spiritual traditions. Then there is Dr. John Montanet who was among Marie's significant influences. Dr. John was born in Africa, lived in Cuba, and then spent much of his life in New Orleans.

Judika Illes

The Weiser Field Guide to
witches

From Hexes to Hermione Granger,
from Salem to the Land of Oz

He is another pivotal, but often unsung hero of occultism. All of these people and more are described in detail in both my *Element Encyclopedia of Witchcraft* and the *Weiser Field Guide to Witches*.

Rumor has it that you are also the author of another Weiser Field Guide.

That's right. *The Weiser Field Guide to the Paranormal* is credited to Judith Joyce – but she's really my alter ego. For a variety of reasons, mainly the brief time span between publication of my two Weiser field guides, that book was credited to an alias, but it's my book. I had a lot of fun writing it. It's a fairly open secret that I wrote that book. One of my favorite reviews was from someone who recognized the consistency of writing styles in my two Weiser field guides.

Can you tell us about your most recent book, Judika?

The Encyclopedia of Mystics, Saints, and Spirits was published by HarperOne in autumn 2011.

My earlier book *The Encyclopedia of Spirits* was originally intended to include angels and saints, as well as a vast variety of Pagan spirits, such as goddesses, fairies, lwa and orishas. But the manuscript became too lengthy and the angels and saints were sidelined in the hopes that someday they each would have their own books. *The Encyclopedia of Mystics, Saints and Sages* includes saints from a wide variety of spiritual traditions. It explores the commonality of saints who are, by definition, the helpful, benevolent, powerful and generous dead – those dead souls who concern themselves with the well-being of the living. Any book on saints will, by necessity, be dominated by Christian saints, just because there are so many more of them – and the encyclopedia explains why this is so. But there are also Jewish saints, Sufi saints, Buddhist saints, Thelemite saints, Zoroastrian saints and a wide variety of folk saints, such as Santa Muerte, Jesus Malverde, and Teresita. There are also modern Pagan saints like Boudica and Hypatia. Certain countries, like Argentina and Vietnam, have a particularly rich variety of folk saints. *The Encyclopedia of Mystics, Saints and Sages*, like *The Encyclopedia of Spirits*, is a very practical book for direct interaction with these sacred beings. With all my books I try to make my topics as concrete and real as I can, rather than speaking in abstractions. In the same way that I want readers to comprehend who Helena Blavatsky, Marie Laveau, the Fox sisters, and Barney and Betty Hill really were as people, I want them to have a sense of Teresa of Avila or the Seven African Powers as real, true beings who coexist in the world with us.

What are your plans for the future?

I have a number of half-finished books in my head that I would someday like to publish. I would really like to publish *Frogs and Pomegranates*, my fertility manuscript, as well as an encyclopedia of angels, which would complete a trilogy with *The Encyclopedias of Spirits* and *Mystics, Saints and Sages*. Plus I really enjoy teaching. I teach workshops on topics like divination, saint veneration, goddess spirituality and all sorts of magical techniques. Over the past decade, I've published four encyclopedias, two field guides and two books devoted to magic spells, so I've spent a considerable amount of time indoors and alone. I'm looking forward to getting out of the house and doing more teaching.

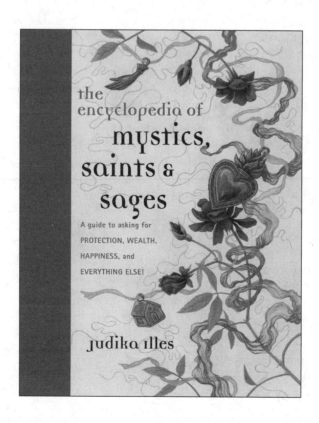

the encyclopedia of

mystics, saints & sages

A guide to asking for
PROTECTION, WEALTH,
HAPPINESS, and
EVERYTHING ELSE!

judika illes

DIAMONDS

Crystals of the Sun

AT ITS brightest and best, the diamond is truly a crystal of the sun. It is the traditional birth stone for those born under the sign of Aries, the zodiac sign in which the sun is at its exaltation. Hold a fine diamond in Sol's light and bright, flashing rainbows of color appear.

Of course, the sun may be either friend or foe. Its light and warmth are the source of all life on Planet Earth, yet excessive sunlight can cause the precious life force to wither and die. In similar fashion, diamonds are reputed to possess great potential for good as well as evil. They are revered as talismans which may either heal or harm.

Metaphysically speaking, diamonds are linked to fidelity, the promise of

pure love, faith, and endurance as well as the manifestation of abundance coupled with the clarity of youthful innocence. Clairvoyants who study variations in the human aura perceive that wearing a diamond helps open inner doors of untapped potential. Wearing diamonds may also induce serenity and encourage the elimination of obstacles. It has even been said that diamonds regenerate the cells of the body.

The King of All Crystals, A Hard-Nosed Rock

In Italian Witchcraft traditions, the diamond is known as the *Amante de Dio*, or a lover of God. This suggests that diamonds, the King of Crystals, facilitates a deeper connection with the divine. Diamonds are a symbol of the richness of the higher self.

The ancient Greek root word *adamas* – the origin of the word diamond – may be translated as "unconquered" and "indestructible." The modern English word *adamant* derives from the same source. Just as a person who is adamant won't give up on a belief, so is the diamond a hard-nosed rock. Made of almost pure carbon, the hardest known substance on Earth, a diamond can only be cut and polished by a tool made of another diamond; hence the phrase "diamond cut diamond."

Splinters of Stars, Divine Teardrops

People have loved and collected diamonds for at least the past four thousand years. Although today they are mined, at first they were simply plucked from river beds. Plato and the Greek philosophers believed that stones were actually alive and that their chemicals would vivify nature devas and astral entities or spirits.

The Greeks saw diamonds as "splinters of stars" or as "teardrops of the gods fallen to Earth." As the beautiful crystals sparkled in the sunlight, they appeared to be magical. Eventually, diamond studded leather breast plates became the first bullet proof vests. Potential assassins would turn away if a diamond was spotted as these stones were suspected of turning malicious actions and evil intent back upon the perpetrators.

Love's True Guardian

Once upon a time, only kings were allowed to own diamonds. By 1300, French and English royalty wore diamonds. When Austrian Archduke Maximilian gave a diamond ring to Maria of Burgundy in 1477, the sparkling stone acquired its reputation as a guardian of pure and indestructible love. Modern suitors still maintain this tradition by presenting diamond rings to their fiancées. This is the origin of the popular axiom "diamonds are a girl's best friend." In sixteenth century England, diamonds were called scribbling rings. It was fashionable for love crazy suitors to etch romantic graffiti on window panes using a diamond ring.

Today's stones are more brilliant than those worn long ago. An example may be seen in an eleventh century diamond crown worn by a Hungarian queen. It is very beautiful, but by modern standards, its stones are dull. The glow of some diamonds, however, is so bright that they are said to confer such desirable virtues as warming the skin; winning law suits; and protecting a garden from blight or lightning. The variety of colors found in diamonds ranges from crystal clear to pink, black, canary yellow, green, red, violet and the very rare and valuable dark blue. Perhaps the different colors provide clues as to variations in the characters or influences of individual stones.

The Curse of the Hope Diamond

Before 1725, most of the world's diamonds came from India, and it is there that in about 1653 that the most sinister and infamous chapter in the intriguing history of diamonds begins: the curse of the Hope Diamond. It is said that the Hope, a huge blue diamond, was originally set in the eye of a statue of the goddess Sita, wife of Rama, the seventh avatar of Vishnu. Sita's diamond eye vanished mysteriously. The identity of the thief has never been confirmed; perhaps the curse begins here.

The diamond resurfaced in France where it was brought – without explanation – by Jean-Baptiste Tavernier, a merchant traveler. A huge triangular stone weighing 115 carats, it was dubbed the Tavernier Blue. Tavernier wrote a book, *Six Voyages,* in which he included several sketches of the unusual and impressive stone. In 1669, Tavernier sold the blue diamond to King Louis XIV of France. It was recut to a 67 carat stone in 1673 by a court jeweler and the king wore it, set in gold, on a ribbon around his neck. During Louis XV's reign it was known as the Blue Diamond of the Crown or the French Blue and became a piece of ceremonial jewelry linked to the Order of the Golden Fleece.

Detained by the Guillotine

During the French Revolution, King Louis XVI and his wife Marie Antoinette attempted to flee France with the French Blue in their possession. When they were permanently delayed by the guillotine, the blue diamond was turned over to the French government, along with other royal jewels. Maybe this is where the legend of the stone being cursed really began.

The French Blue was stolen during a week of looting in September 1792. In 1812, it mysteriously surfaced once again in London in the possession of a British diamond merchant, one Daniel Eliason. Soon England's King George IV acquired the French Blue. After

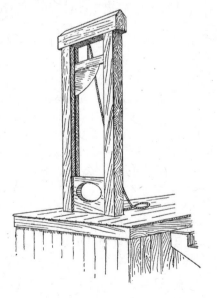

George IV's death in 1830, the diamond was sold through private channels in an attempt to satisfy some of his enormous debts. Its next owner was Henry Philip Hope, the man whose name is associated with the Hope Diamond to this day.

No record documents how Hope acquired the gem or how much he paid for it, but he died in 1839, soon after it came into his possession. The diamond was at the center of much litigation before it was finally inherited by his nephew, Henry Thomas Hope. Later it was passed on to his grandson, Lord Francis Hope. By 1901, Lord Francis was in deep financial trouble. He and his sisters collaborated to sell the stone to pay off some of their debts. A London dealer kept it only briefly before selling it to Joseph Frankels and Sons of New York City. Soon they too desperately needed cash. In 1909, the Hope Diamond changed hands several times, sold first to Selim Habib who put it up for auction in Paris. C.H. Roseanau bought it and resold it almost immediately to Pierre Cartier.

An Angry Goddess

It was about this time that the legend of the gem carrying a curse gained notoriety. Some describe this legend as a Victorian fantasy. A mystery or curse was just a concocted story to make the diamond more appealing to prospective purchasers. Others considered the aura of evil to be real, supposing that the Goddess Sita was displeased about the theft of her eye. In any event, it does seem that most of the Hope Diamond's various owners suffered from bad luck, ranging from bankruptcy to sudden death.

In 1910, the Hope was shown to Mrs. Evalyn Walsh McClean of Washington DC, during a visit to France. Tantalized by the story of the curse, she was drawn to the lovely gem. However she did not care for its setting. Cartier reset it as a tiara in a three-tiered circle with white diamonds. He brought it to the United States for a visit and left it with Mrs. McClean for a weekend.

Cartier's strategy worked. Mrs. McClean found the Hope impossible to resist. She purchased it and wore it with unabashed flamboyance until her death in 1947. It was during these years that the Hope was reset again as the spectacular pendant we recognize today.

A Series of Tragedies

A series of tragedies, including the death of her son, beset Evalyn Walsh McClean during her long tenure of ownership. Was this just the unhappy course that her life would have taken anyway or did the Hope somehow generate tragedies through its curse? Alternatively, were others merely envious of the wealthy socialite and all too ready to comfort themselves by looking for the presence of negativity in the magnificent blue diamond?

In 1949, the New York jeweler, Harry Winston purchased Mrs. McClean's jewelry collection from her estate. By then, the Hope Diamond was so famous – or infamous – that for the next decade it was the star attraction at many exhibits and charity events sponsored by Winston for the Court of Jewels show. Inexplicably, on November 10, 1958, Harry Winston donated the Hope Diamond, deemed to be worth between 200 and 250 million dollars, to the Smithsonian Institution in Washington, D.C.

The Hope Diamond possesses a timeless magnetic draw. Although there are many spectacular gems in the Smithsonian's National Gemstone collections, the Hope immediately became its premier attraction. Millions of visitors each year know the charismatic Hope Diamond by name. Most will merely glance at the other gems as they make the pilgrimage to marvel at it and wonder about the curse it might carry. The Hope's blue color comes from trace amounts of boron within its crystalline structure. It assumes an eerie red glow beneath ultraviolet light. Does the large diamond really emit, as reputed, a subtle energy that debilitates those who claim possession and get too close? Perhaps.

– GRANIA LING

Doll-in-the-Grass

Love Conquers Size

ONCE UPON a time a certain king had a certain whim. Kings do tend to have whims and sometimes, now-and-then, once-in-a-blue-moon the whims are reasonable. This particular whim began reasonably enough. When his twelve sons were grown, the king decreed that they should go into the world and find themselves wives. But he commanded also that each bride must be able to weave, spin and sew a shirt in a day or he would not have her for a daughter-in-law. Who can fathom the profound mind of kings?

The monarch wished his sons good spouse questing and gave each prince a horse and a coat of mail. The princes set out together and had gone some distance when they declared that they would not allow Boots, the youngest brother, to quest with them. "You are a good-for-nothing, fit for nothing," they told him. "Princes are the superstars of the realm, and you just embarrass your royal kin." And to put it as kindly as possible, we have to report with some sorrow that Boots was indeed a bit of a simpleton.

The young prince, abandoned at roadside by his brothers, was shattered. He had no idea what to do or where to go next. Boots dismounted, sat down in the tall grass and wept in confusion. Suddenly tufts of grass rustled, stirred, and there appeared a charming miniature of a girl. Boots was astounded. "Would you like to come with me and meet Doll-in-the-Grass?" she asked. Overcome with curiosity, Boots agreed.

The odd couple

Doll-in-the-Grass was sitting on a chair of fragrant rosemary, wearing a dress woven of violets. She was a figure as big as your thumb, as beautiful as a summer morning, as smart as ten professors in a row. "Why are you weeping?" she asked. Boots told her that his brothers had forsaken him at roadside and that he was in quest of a bride that could spin, weave and sew a shirt in a day. "If you can do that, it will be my happiness to make you my wife," he declared, dazzled by her lovely form, tiny as it was. Did I mention that what Boots lacked in brains he embodied in heart? Doll-in-the-Grass recognized the loving nature of the prince and agreed. At a dizzying speed she spun, she wove and she sewed a perfect little shirt with buttons so small as to be invisible, for the shirt was only the size of half a thumb.

Boots set off with it back to the castle, apprehensive of what his father would think of the shirtlet. But the king chuckled at the charm and wit of the garment and gave his permission for his son to wed its maker, however odd her size. Boots returned at a gallop, thrilled to claim his little sweetheart and bring her back to the castle as his bride.

The couple rejoiced at their meeting, and the prince tried to scoop her up to ride before him on his saddle. But Doll-in-the-Grass insisted on her own way to go. "I have my own carriage and horses," she said proudly. The "carriage" was a silver spoon, the "horses" little white mice with reins of silken thread. Boots rode on the opposite side of the road, fearful of crushing his bride, she was so little.

Eleven ugly brides

When they came to a river, Boots's horse, spooked by the water, reared and upset the spoon. Doll-in-the-Grass was hurled into the water and sank. Boots plunged into the river and fished around, hoping to find her and pull her out. But he found no trace of his beloved and finally threw himself down on the river bank, in shock, heartbroken. Suddenly the water roiled and a merman surfaced with a lady in his arms – Doll-in-the-Grass, wet, shiny, of human size and lovelier now than ever. The merman waved his tail and vanished.

Boots took his bride up on his saddle and rode home with her. All his brothers had returned with their ugly brides, who had been quarreling all the way home. Each carried an ill-made shirt already falling apart at the seams. When his brothers saw Boots's beautiful bride, they burst with jealousy and began to attack him. The king was so dismayed at his nasty new family that he drove away the eleven brothers and eleven brides and destroyed the eleven raggedy shirts. He gave Boots and Doll-in-the-Grass a beautiful wedding feast. Then, the old Norse tale assures us, "they lived well and happily together a long, long time, and if they're not dead, why, they're alive still."

– BARBARA STACY
Adapted from Popular Tales from the Norse, *by Peter Christen Asbjornsen and Jorgen Moe*

Charles Godfrey Leland

Guiding Light of the Modern Witchcraft Revival

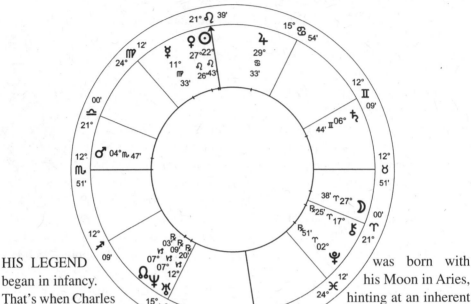

HIS LEGEND began in infancy. That's when Charles Godfrey Leland attended his first secret ritual. Leland, who has long been hailed as the founding father of modern witchcraft, was born on August 15, 1824 in Philadelphia, Pennsylvania. A mysterious nurse who was in attendance at the birth whisked the newborn away to the attic of the family's Philadelphia home. There she performed a ceremony upon him. The specifics have been lost, but it involved a Bible, a key, a knife, salt, coins, and candle light. She pronounced that baby Charles would have a long life and become a "scholar and a wizard." His fascination with magical folk traditions was foreshadowed.

The Moon rules early childhood and family life in the horoscope. Leland was born with his Moon in Aries, hinting at an inherent spirit of innovation and an affinity for being a pioneer. His Moon was separating from a wide conjunction with both Chiron and Pluto. This pattern reveals intensity, hidden depths, and a yen for adventure and knowledge. The Aries Moon favorably trines both Venus and the Sun in Leo. A Sun–Moon trine is associated with great good luck and health; astrologers sometimes call this the "darling of the gods" aspect. The Sun and Venus conjunct in flamboyant, dramatic, and proud Leo reveal Leland's affinity for the fine arts and his attractive persona. His Mercury, dignified in its own ruling sign of Virgo, shows inherent intelligence, ability with languages, and a grasp of detail. Mercury is further strengthened by a trine to his Neptune, north node, and Uranus conjunction in Capricorn.

Neptune is especially associated with magic and psychic phenomena, while Uranus adds sparkle and originality.

Leland was a child of wealth and privilege. His father, Charles Leland Sr., and his mother, Charlotte Godfrey, were successful commission merchants. Leland's Jupiter, the planet of wealth, is exalted in Cancer, sign of home and heritage. He attended Princeton University, where he excelled as a poet and linguist. Saturn, the hard work indicator in the birth chart, is in mobile, versatile Gemini. This describes Leland's many talents as well as his productive travels.

While living in Heidelberg and Munich, Leland adopted the pen name of Hans Breitmann and published poetry in both English and German. His popular verse *Jasmine Valentine* reveals his sensitive side and his ability to capture romantic imagery.

Among the flowers no perfume is
  like mine;
That which is best in me comes
  from within.
So those in this world who would
  rise and shine
Should seek internal excellence
  to win.
And though 'tis true that
  falsehood and despair
Meet in my name, yet
  bear it still in mind
That where they meet
  they perish. All is fair
When they are gone and
  nought remains behind.

During the 1840's, Leland fulfilled the promise of his Saturn in Gemini by pursuing a wide variety of other interests and studies, including Hermeticism and Neo-Platonism. While at the Sorbonne in Paris, he fulfilled the promise of his Mars – traditionally considered the planet of war and conflict – which fell in Scorpio, its sign of co-rulership. Charles became a revolutionary. As a soldier, he fought against the king's army, constructing barricades. A powerful Scorpio influence inevitably indicates secrets and hidden aspects. According to Leland's biographers, this coincides with the time period when he was first labeled a "Romany Rye" – or a "Friend of the Gypsies." This association was to be a background theme throughout the rest of his long life. The free-wheeling Gypsies (Romany) are traditionally linked astrologically to Uranus, the eccentric and independent planet, which is so strongly emphasized in Leland's natal chart.

When the money his father had given him for travel ran out, Leland returned to Pennsylvania, where he passed the bar exam. However, a career in law did not appeal to him and he soon turned to journalism as a source of income. While writing for several publications, including *The Illustrated News of New York*, he was offered editorships at *Graham's Magazine* and *Philadelphia Press*. He honed his writing skills to perfection and developed a reputation for whimsical, appealing pen-and-ink drawings. In years to come, readers of his books about witchcraft would cherish this distinctive art. In 1856 Leland married Eliza Bella "Isabel" Fischer. Their union was a happy one. The two remained devoted to each other.

In 1857, while he was editor of *Graham's Magazine*, Leland published his German dialect poem, *Hans Breitmann's Party*, which became so popular that he composed others, leading to the publication of *Hans Breitmann's Ballads* in 1869. He founded and edited the *Continental Monthly* in Boston in 1862 to further the Union cause. In the 1880s, he also successfully introduced industrial and craft arts into American schools. The great Oscar Wilde wrote to Leland and – paying tribute to Leland's contributions to art education – stated that he would be "recognised and honoured as one of the great pioneers and leaders of the art of the future."

After more than thirty years of living in the United States, Leland suddenly returned to Europe. In 1888, when he was 64 years of age, he turned up in Florence, Italy. It was here that fate would intervene and Leland would begin what many consider the most significant of his contributions. Leland met a card reader and fortune teller named Maddalena Taluti, a practitioner

 from the back alleys of Florence. Leland's natal Mars in Scorpio is in a quincunx aspect to both his Saturn in Gemini and his Pluto in Aries. This is a complex and unusual star pattern which astrologers call a Yod, also known as either the Eye or the Finger of God. Those born with a Yod are guided by fate. Unplanned forces outside the norm take a hand in shaping their lives.

Following the fateful meeting with Maddalena, Leland began to research and record an ancient witchcraft tradition. This was published in his landmark work *Aradia, Gospel of the Witches* (1899). Until his death in 1903, Leland cultivated contacts with traditional and hereditary witches throughout Europe.

Leland wrote more than 50 other books, including *The English Gypsies* (1873), *Gypsy Sorcery and Fortune Telling* (1891), *The Hundred Riddles of the Fairy Bellaria* (1892) and *The Witchcraft of Dame Darrel of York* (2011).

Charles Leland

Charles Godfrey Leland was born on August 15, 1824
in Philadelphia, Pennsylvania

39° 57' N / 75° 09' W
A noon-style chart is used
as the exact birth time is unknown

Data Table

(Tropical Placidus House Cusps)

Sun 22 Leo 43 – 10th house

Moon 27 Aries 38 – 6th house

Mercury 11 Virgo 33 – 10th house

Venus 27 Leo 26 – 10th house

Mars 4 Scorpio 47 – 12th house

Jupiter 29 Cancer 33 – 9th house

Saturn 6 Gemini 44 – 7th house

Uranus 12 Capricorn 20 (retrograde) – 2nd house

Neptune 7 Capricorn 09 (retrograde) – 2nd house

Pluto 2 Aries 51 (retrograde) – 2nd house

N. Moon Node 7 Capricorn 03 – 2nd house

Chiron 17 Aries 25 (retrograde) – 5th house

Ascendant (Rising Sign) is Scorpio

COMEDY AND TRAGEDY UNMASKED

Faces of Humanity in the
Silent Messages of Janus

THEIR WORDLESS message is profound. It may encompass the entire gamut of the human experience. Silently they observe, from across the centuries, simultaneously repelling and beckoning. Grinning and grimacing, with distorted and exaggerated and vaguely human features, the faces touch upon something sinister or even grotesque. For hundreds of years – at least since Shakespeare's time – the Comedy and Tragedy masks have been the exclusive symbol of creative artistry, especially theater. The power of drama to explain the human condition is shown by these dual images of joy and despair.

These masks first appeared in Athens about 600 BCE, during the golden age of ancient Greece, when the first plays were written. Performances were originally rituals of magic, intended to honor and invoke Dionysus, the god of procreation and life, revelry and fertility, who gave both comedies and tragedies as a gift to humanity.

The earliest of these stylized masks were large, to communicate either good or bad humor over the vast distances of amphitheaters that might accommodate audiences of 10,000. By watching the masks, those sitting in the 'cheap seats' could follow the story. All of the actors were male and had to assume multiple roles. The mouths on the masks were wide to aid in projecting the voice. The masks were like body shields, costumes in themselves, held by performers who were barely clothed. Made of clay, wood and linen, the masks were the real stars of these early theatricals. Masks allowed characters to be recognized and understood from afar.

The Genesis of Thespians

The traditional comedy and tragedy masks illustrated how a play's protagonist and antagonist – the main characters – would interact with the chorus. Legends tell that a playwright named Thespias of Attica first added these stars, who then wore the faces of Comedy and Tragedy. The term "Thespian" was coined in his honor and has been used ever since to refer to serious actors.

Thespias' first stories described

the dual-edged impact of sacred wine. The ebullient aspects of wine were considered Comedy, while the darker, anguished-filled harvesting of grapes was Tragedy. The masks show truth of expression – how hidden desires surface to fearlessly reveal human nature. They allowed release from conformity, while simultaneously assuring anonymity.

The presence of the nine Muses, goddesses who guide all creative expression, was also shown through the beloved happy-sad masks. Melpomene, the Muse of Tragedy, would enter with the sad face, while Thalia, Muse of Comedy, wore the happy one. These twin or balanced genres create a kind of catharsis, enabling the audience to find healing. Human nature hasn't changed much. People today still experience the same satisfaction when they become absorbed in a good movie, play, or opera.

The Two-Faced God

Another name for these enduring symbols is Janus Masks. The reference to the Roman god Janus was born when the Romans adopted these masks. Janus, who gives his name to the month January, has two faces. One looks to the future, while the other gazes back toward the past. The two-faced symbol of Janus was placed in doorways to guard both the inside and outside of a dwelling. Janus was also the god who opened and closed doors. He watched over the beginnings and endings of events. These duties were symbolized by the appearance of his two faces on curtains that would open and close at the beginning and end of a theatrical production.

The Greeks apparently preferred comedy, but since Shakespeare's time tragedy has been considered the more impressive of the arts. The Janus masks are usually shown linked by a ribbon, indicating their interdependence. They need each other, forever bound by common roots and ties. Both are essential in expressing the complex dramas of life and art.

– ESTHER ELAYNE

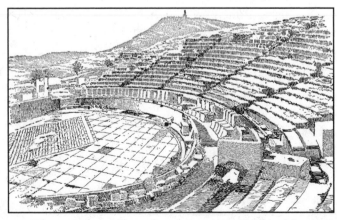

Dionysus Theatre. One of the earliest open-air theaters in Athens, Greece.

97

the cluRichaun

A Meeting with the Leprechauns' Surly Cousin

ONE NIGHT, near Lammas, not so long ago, one Felix O'Driscoll had a wee bit too much to drink at a pub in Ireland. He began to debate with a lady, a Ms. Fitzpatrick, about the fairies. She was shocked when O'Driscoll shouted aloud that he thought the Little People were a load of nonsense and stated that he especially didn't believe in the clurichaun (kloor-a-kawn). All the tales about them, he added, were the greatest load of foolishness.

This attracted the attention of all the patrons in the pub. In Ireland, it is widely considered most unwise to deny the existence of the fey folk. Everyone gathered around to hear how the conversation would go. The lady shouted back that there were certainly clurichauns because her own father – an honest man if ever there was one – had met one. She offered this account of the event.

An Honest Father's Tale

It was a fine evening in late summer when her father, Thomas Fitzpatrick, saw a tiny brown jug, as he strolled near a hedge. Curious, he took a closer look, and saw a little man perched on a stool, holding two more jugs, one in each hand. Without taking his eyes away, Thomas wished the clurichaun good afternoon and asked what was in the jugs. The wee one answered civilly, saying that it was a good beer made from heather tops, adding that the recipe had been taught to his great great-grandparents by some visiting Danes and had been kept a family secret ever since. As a pretext, Thomas asked for a taste. He then grabbed the clurichaun and asked where his gold was hidden. The wee one wriggled and made a face. He advised Thomas to be getting along home, as his cows had broken through his fence and were trampling the neighbor's field. Thomas almost turned away, but then he remembered the wiliness of the clurichaun. He insisted upon being shown the gold. The two debated a while, but Thomas stood his ground and held on tight.

Finally, the clurichaun obliged. He led Thomas over rough country, for a very long distance. At last, they came to a vast field of ragwort plants. Pointing to one of the plants, the clurichaun said that all the gold Thomas could ever

want was buried right there. Thomas was delighted, but said he had to go and get his shovel. The exhausted clurichaun lit his tiny pipe and pleaded to be set free, as he was no longer needed. He was so tired, he added. Being a kind-hearted gentleman, Thomas agreed. He tied a red scarf around the money plant and then hurried home. When Thomas returned with the shovel, the clurichaun was nowhere to be seen. And every plant in the vast field had identical pieces of red cloth tied to it.

Tippling Leprechauns

Clurichauns are mainly found in County Cork. They are small, about two feet high, with grey wrinkled skin and red noses. Always drunk, their great loves are tobacco and spirits – especially heather ale and whiskey. They enjoy riding on sheep and dogs during moon-lit nights. The clurichauns are solitary folk. Their typical attire includes old fashion tri-cornered or pointed hats (which they have been known to use as weapons), red swallow-tailed evening coats with large silver buttons, red breeches, blue or grey stockings, and high heeled shoes with buckles. The more sociable leprechauns usually dress in green.

Some say that clurichauns are merely leprechauns on a drinking spree. It has also been rumored that leprechauns – who diligently work all day as expert cobblers – change into clurichauns after hours. This just isn't true. The two types of wee folk are far too different to be one and the same. Although both are expert con artists and their names are derived from a common Middle Irish root word meaning a "sprite", the clurichauns have completely different priorities and personalities than their more sober cousins.

Guardians of Fine Wine and Precious Spirits

The leprechaun presents himself as a kind of jovial banker or cobbler. Industrious and prosperous, leprechauns are usually observed working as fast as they can to finish a single shoe. Leprechauns are greedy for gold, and have been spotted carrying a pot filled with it to hide at the end of the rainbow.

Clurichauns are wealthy, too, but, rather than laboring, they prefer to frequent wine cellars, acting as self appointed guardians of fine liquors. In character, clurichauns are rather manic depressive. One minute, they are singing and whistling like affable drunks and, then, in a twinkling, they turn sullen and morose. They have been known to be helpful, attaching themselves to households to scare any dishonest servants who attempt to steal the wine.

The Clurichaun's Cousins

The magic of the clurichaun is at its most powerful when Lammas is celebrated. That's when the ingredients for

the various ales, wines and liquors are ready to harvest. The first potatoes are ready to dig, there are plenty of hops, heather blossoms, and the many fruits of autumn are sweet and fresh.

Other cousins of the clurichaun include the sinister Fir Darrig of Donegal – a feared and macabre practical joker; as well as the more provincial Loghery Man of Ulster, and the Lurigadaune of Tipperary and Luricane of Kerry. Seemingly, no female members of this extended leprechaun family have ever been observed.

– GRANIA LING

Margo Miller (1936 – 2001), was the dear friend and great astrologer who first introduced this author to the Clurichaun. This account of The Little People is lovingly dedicated to her memory.

Here is a contemporary version of the potent and traditional British heather ale recipe attributed to the clurichaun. A basic list of ingredients is given. For specific brewing methods, please consult a step-by-step guide.

ḃeaṪḣer aⱡe

20 liters of un-chlorinated water
1.8 kg pale malt extract
350g caramel malt
120g roasted barley
1 kg Maris Otter pale malt
250g Munich malt
30g Pacific Gem bittering hop
30g Kent Goldings finishing hops
30g Hallertaur Mittlefrueh finishing hops
250g fresh heather tips yeast
(for example: Wyeast 1318 London Ale III style or 1728 Scottish Ale)
For bottling add 200ml malt extract

GETTYSBURG

America's Ghost Hunting Paradise

GETTYSBURG, the Civil War battle with the greatest number of casualties, began on July 1, 1863, the day of a Full Moon. For three days, the furious battle – immortalized in President Abraham Lincoln's famous "Gettysburg Address" – raged. Its cannonade has been described as the most horrific ever. It should perhaps then be no surprise that so many serious paranormal investigators consider Gettysburg, Pennsylvania to be their very favorite among all the haunted places in the United States.

Some eyewitness accounts of the Battle of Gettysburg survive. Captain Robert Carter, a Union soldier, recalled, "It is said that the roar, the jar, was heard in Philadelphia, over 80 miles away." George Clark of the Confederacy recorded that "the noise and din were so furious, so overwhelming, as well as continuous, that one had to scream to his neighbor beside him to be heard at all …men could be seen bleeding at both ears from concussion." Perhaps J. H. Moore of the 7th Tennessee summed it all up best with his remarks,

"No imagination can adequately conceive of the magnitude of artillery duel. It surpassed the ordinary battle fire as the earthquake surpasses the muttering of an ordinary thunderstorm." Yet another Confederate soldier added, "Grim-visaged war had never before assumed a more hideous face."

An Eerie Quiet in the Summer's Heat

Many of those killed at Gettysburg were rendered unrecognizable. One Virginian wrote in his diary, "In many instances the bodies were literally torn to pieces. Here lay a body without a head. Arms and legs were separated from the trunks to which they belonged, or so mutilated and rent that it would have been hard to place those scattered fragments of humanity in the proper places."

When the shots finally ceased, an eerie quiet settled over the carnage. The smoke hovered in the summer's heat. Over 50,000 soldiers and a single civilian, a beautiful young woman, lay dead. Dying in the full bloom of youth, their vital young lives torn from them, their spirits are forever restless and can easily be sensed. To this very day, some are heard or observed meandering through the battle fields or setting up encampments. Tourists who insist that they have witnessed Civil War reenactments are regularly told that none occurred at the time. Instead, what these visitors are really seeing is what is known as "residual haunting": ghost soldiers battle repeatedly and seemingly eternally in very haunted Gettysburg.

Séance Rooms and Mourning Parlors

Gettysburg, this small and picturesque historical town, is surrounded by park-like battlefields and, of course, a huge cemetery. A quick internet search reveals many fascinating sites of interest. At least a dozen different ghost tours are offered. It's possible to walk with a costumed tour guide by lantern light and hear beautifully narrated ghost stories. Late night jaunts with high tech ghost tracking equipment intended to verify the presence of ghosts are quite marvelous. A Civil War-era séance room offers demonstrations of Victorian-style communication with the afterlife. A mourning parlor located in a damp stone walled cellar displays 19th century funeral accoutrements. Phenomena may be observed while ghostly lore is shared by knowledgeable Gettysburg residents.

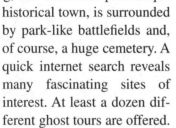

One of the many heartwrenching stories of the Battle of Gettysburg involves the Civil War Soldiers' Children's Orphanage. One soldier died clutching a photo of his three children, but none of the survivors knew his name. This photo was published in newspapers, circulating throughout the nation. The soldier's widow saw it and came forward. She and the children had no source of support and were homeless. She was offered the position as the first matron of the orphanage, built across the street from a battlefield and next to the cemetery. A ghost tour is now offered there at night, when the forlorn spirits of some of the orphans visit, still seeking the parents who never returned for them.

The Ghost of Jennie Wade

Jennie Wade, age 20, the sole civilian and the only woman killed during the conflict, is believed likely to also be the first casualty of the Battle of Gettysburg. On the morning of July 1, when tensions were building, and the conflict was about to erupt, Jennie was making bread at her sister's home. Ironically, Jennie had left her own downtown home, a short distance away, because she was afraid to stay there: she felt safer on the outskirts of Gettysburg. Jennie's mother was there, too, helping, as the sister had just given birth.

At the sound of the first shots, Jennie opened an interior door in the kitchen behind the front door and stood behind it to knead her dough, confident that she would be protected because she was away from the windows and protected behind the two doors. Suddenly, a single bullet pierced both the front and kitchen doors, striking Jennie in the back, killing her instantly.

Her heartbroken family carried Jennie's body into the cellar. Jennie's mother finished baking the bread and fed it to the soldiers, who were nearly starving. This isn't the end of Jennie's story, though. She was engaged to be married. The family wondered how to get word to her fiancé, a soldier stationed in another area. Then a letter arrived. The fiancé had been killed in combat at almost exactly the same time as Jennie was struck down. Today, the Jennie Wade House is a museum and offers ghost hunts. Jennie's wooden bread trough is on display. Paranormal investigations conducted there have observed phenomena all over the property.

Denied her own happy marriage, Jennie's spirit now intervenes to help other hopeful brides-to-be. The legend is that when a single lady who desires marriage slips her wedding ring finger – the third finger of her left hand – through the hole left by the fatal bullet and simultaneously wishes for a marriage proposal, she will receive it within one year. The curator of the Jennie Wade House Museum proudly displays a book of letters and bridal photos from visitors, documenting Jennie's wonderful gift from the beyond.

– MARINA BRYONY

Moon Cycles

A New Moon rises with the Sun,
Her waxing half at midday shows,
The Full Moon climbs at sunset hour,
And waning half the midnight knows.

NEW 2013	FULL	NEW 2014	FULL
January 11	January 26	January 1, 30	January 15
February 10	February 25	February – none	February 14
March 11	March 27	March 1, 30	March 16
April 10	April 25	April 29	April 15
May 9	May 25	May 28	May 14
June 8	June 23	June 27	June 12
July 8	July 22	July 26	July 12
August 6	August 20	August 25	August 10
September 5	September 19	September 24	September 8
October 4	October 18	October 23	October 8
November 3	November 17	November 22	November 6
December 2	December 17	December 21	December 6

Life takes on added dimension when you
match your activities to the waxing and waning of the Moon.
Observe the sequence of her phases to learn
the wisdom of constant change within complete certainty.

presage

by Dikki-Jo Mullen

ARIES 2012 — PISCES 2013

SOLAR RADIATION sent to Earth by the Sun is vital to life as we know it. When this changes by the tiniest bit, the impact is profound. The Sun has begun this second decade of the 21st century by periodically blowing its top, generating heightened radiation with sunspot and solar flare activity. The wise will heed news of these celestial events and remember to keep a cool head. When the Sun acts up there is a correlation with cycles of political unrest, violent crime, and extreme weather. Everyone is a bit jittery and even the most mild-mannered can express anger.

Discover where your Sun shines by starting with your familiar Sun or birth sign. Next consider your Moon and rising signs. The Moon relates to emotional needs and helps in processing memories. The rising sign or ascendant describes the physical self, the side you present to the world. The eclipses and retrogrades section presents information about cycles which have a more universal effect.

The spirituality sections refer to esoteric ruler and mission statements. These delve beyond the illusions and concerns of the everyday (exoteric) world. The esoteric or spiritual ruler of your birth sign might be different from the familiar one.

In the finance sections of Presage the Earth signs are mentioned. Earth is always the zodiac sign directly across from the familiar Sun sign and describes the path to healthy grounding. Astrology holds the key to feeling more content and spiritually in tune while pursuing success in a rapidly changing world.

More detailed information about Esoteric Astrology and the Earth Signs is available in the Almanac Extras section at www.TheWitchesAlmanac.com.

ASTROLOGICAL KEYS

Signs of the Zodiac
Channels of Expression

ARIES: fiery, pioneering, competitive
TAURUS: earthy, stable, practical
GEMINI: dual, lively, versatile
CANCER: protective, traditional
LEO: dramatic, flamboyant, warm
VIRGO: conscientious, analytical
LIBRA: refined, fair, sociable
SCORPIO: intense, secretive, ambitious
SAGITTARIUS: friendly, expansive
CAPRICORN: cautious, materialistic
AQUARIUS: inquisitive, unpredictable
PISCES: responsive, dependent, fanciful

Elements

FIRE: Aries, Leo, Sagittarius
EARTH: Taurus, Virgo, Capricorn
AIR: Gemini, Libra, Aquarius
WATER: Cancer, Scorpio, Pisces

Qualities

CARDINAL	FIXED	MUTABLE
Aries	Taurus	Gemini
Cancer	Leo	Virgo
Libra	Scorpio	Sagittarius
Capricorn	Aquarius	Pisces

CARDINAL signs mark the beginning of each new season — active.
FIXED signs represent the season at its height — steadfast.
MUTABLE signs herald a change of season — variable.

Celestial Bodies
Generating Energy of the Cosmos

Sun: birth sign, ego, identity
Moon: emotions, memories, personality
Mercury: communication, intellect, skills
Venus: love, pleasures, the fine arts
Mars: energy, challenges, sports
Jupiter: expansion, religion, happiness
Saturn: responsibility, maturity, realities
Uranus: originality, science, progress
Neptune: dreams, illusions, inspiration
Pluto: rebirth, renewal, resources

Glossary of Aspects

Conjunction: two planets within the same sign or less than 10 degrees apart, favorable or unfavorable according to the nature of the planets.

Sextile: a pleasant, harmonious aspect occurring when two planets are two signs or 60 degrees apart.

Square: a major negative effect resulting when planets are three signs from one another or 90 degrees apart.

Trine: planets four signs or 120 degrees apart, forming a positive and favorable influence.

Quincunx: a mildly negative aspect produced when planets are five signs or 150 degrees apart.

Opposition: a six sign or 180 degrees separation of planets generating positive or negative forces depending on the planets involved.

The Houses — *Twelve Areas of Life*

1st house: appearance, image, identity
2nd house: money, possessions, tools
3rd house: communications, siblings
4th house: family, domesticity, security
5th house: romance, creativity, children
6th house: daily routine, service, health
7th house: marriage, partnerships, union
8th house: passion, death, rebirth, soul
9th house: travel, philosophy, education
10th house: fame, achievement, mastery
11th house: goals, friends, high hopes
12th house: sacrifice, solitude, privacy

Eclipses

Eclipses generate changes and surprises. A birthday within three days of an eclipse augurs a time of growth. There will be four eclipses this year. A total eclipse is more influential than a partial.

May 20, 2012 New Moon Solar in Gemini, south node – partial
June 4, 2012 Full Moon Lunar in Sagittarius, north node – partial
November 13, 2012 New Moon Solar in Scorpio, north node – total
November 28, 2012 Full Moon Lunar in Gemini, south node – partial

Retrograde Planetary Motion

The illusion of apparent backward planetary motion is created by the Earth's speed relative to the other planets. Astrologically it assures a change of pace.

Mercury Retrograde Cycle
Retrograde Mercury affects technology, travel, and communication. Those who have been out of touch return. Complete old projects, revise, review, and tread familiar paths. Gemini and Virgo will be affected.

March 13–April 5, 2012
in Aries and Pisces
July 15–August 9, 2012 in Leo
November 7–27, 2012
in Sagittarius and Scorpio
February 24–March 18, 2013 in Pisces

Venus Retrograde Cycle
Venus retrograde influences art, love, and finances. Taurus and Libra will be affected.

May 16–June 28, 2012 in Gemini

Mars Retrograde Cycle
The military, sports, and heavy industry are impacted. Aries will be affected.

January 24–April 14, 2012 in Virgo

Jupiter Retrograde Cycle
Large animals, speculation, education, and religion are impacted. Sagittarius is affected.

October 5, 2012–January 31, 2013
in Gemini

Saturn Retrograde Cycle
Elderly people, the disadvantaged, employment, and natural resources are linked to Saturn. Capricorn will be affected.

February 7, 2012–June 26, 2012
in Libra
February 19, 2013–July 8, 2013
in Scorpio

Uranus Retrograde Cycle
Inventions, science, electronics, revolutionaries, and extreme weather relate to Uranus retrograde. Aquarius is impacted.

July 14–December 14, 2012 in Aries

Neptune Retrograde Cycle
Water, aquatic creatures, chemicals, and psychic phenomena are impacted by Neptune retrograde. Pisces will be affected.

June 5–November 12, 2012 in Pisces

Pluto Retrograde Cycle
Ecology, espionage, birth and death rates, nuclear power, and mysteries relate to Pluto retrograde. Scorpio will be influenced.

April 11–September 19, 2012 in
Capricorn

ARIES
The year ahead for those
born under the sign of the Ram
March 20–April 19

The promise of new challenges characterizes this Mars-ruled celestial warrior. Courage, an upfront approach to activities, and a tendency to abandon a project once it's begun to chase a fresh challenge can be expected from the zodiac's first sign. This trait is both a blessing and a liability to the Ram.

The New Moon Aries on March 22 favors Ostara rituals to empower new ventures. Select goals. Moving on is the keynote. It's a perfect time to forgive and forget. Until April 14 Mars is retrograde in your 6th house, affecting both your own energy level and the well-being of animal companions. Postpone welcoming a new pet into the household until later in the year. Mid-April through May 9 Mercury moves rapidly through your sign. Plans for travel and study progress. It's an optimum time for problem solving.

As Midsummer's Day approaches, your 3rd house is strong. A neighbor sincerely expresses concern and friendship. Casual conversations offer unexpected pearls of wisdom. Ask questions, collect data, and respond to invitations. Current events provide valuable perspectives on your personal situation. At the July 4th holiday, Mars joins Saturn in your sector of relationships, a trend lasting through August 23. Loved ones require more support and attention. There may be a turning point regarding a commitment. Double-check rules and regulations. Questions of legalities and ethics can arise. From just after Lammastide through September 6, Venus brightens your home and family sector. Affectionate devotion shown by loved ones makes meeting their needs more than worthwhile. The late summer is an ideal time to pursue home improvement projects or to make changes regarding living arrangements.

On September 29, the powerful Harvest Moon is in Aries. The lunation conjoins Uranus and squares Pluto. Reflect on how you direct energy and your true desires. There may be a compulsion toward immediate action. A major shift in outlook and priorities can occur during the four weeks following this pattern. From October 7–November 16, Mars moves through Sagittarius, your sister fire sign, forming a very favorable trine aspect to your Sun, stimulating great motivation and accomplishment. A total solar eclipse on November 13 activates your 8th house of mysteries. A subtle message from a loved one who has passed on brings a sense of peace concerning the afterlife. This could involve a vivid dream. As December's days darken and Yuletide nears, your sector of career success becomes increasingly prominent. Pluto is influential. Expect competition and power shifts at work. Honor your personal ambitions. After December 25, any lingering anger will dissipate regarding a difficult associate.

On January 1, Mercury moves to cross your midheaven, followed by Venus on January 9. Supportive friends and new information help realize a cherished goal or enhanced professional status by Candlemas.

Mars joins Neptune in your 12th house from February 2 – March 13. Venus and retrograde Mercury weave into the pattern during late winter. This planetary combination favors craft workings done in complete secrecy. The mantra "power shared is power lost" provides a valuable reminder. Honor the wilderness.

March 14–20 promises a complete change of pace. Cardinal sign influences highlighted by Uranus are active. You'll feel restless and be driven by a desire for adventure. New technologies intrigue you and a revolutionary spirit prevails during winter's final days. Begin an exercise program in anticipation of your 2013 birthday.

HEALTH

While Mars is retrograde in early spring, pay attention to repetitive health patterns and your family's health history. March – April 2012 is a good time to correct destructive health habits. In the autumn, appreciate animal companions. Fostering close ties with a special pet at the autumnal equinox assures nurturing and healing energies which add to your own well-being.

LOVE

The Sun rules the 5th house of love. Sunlight has a potent effect upon your romantic inclinations. Stroll with one you love along a sunny beach or enjoy a beautiful sunrise or sunset together to facilitate an idyllic relationship. September 7 – October 3: Venus brightens your love sector. Saturn moves out of opposition to your Sun on October 6. If a loved one is ill, troubled, or high maintenance, the situation should improve as autumn ends.

SPIRITUALITY

Mercury is the spiritual and esoteric ruler of your sign. The description of your spiritual mission is "I come forth and from the plane of mind I rule." Metaphysical literature and discussion groups help to awaken spirituality. Retrograde Mercury cycles are wonderful times for you to move away from the material realm and explore spiritual principles. The Mercury retrograde of July 15 – August 9 is especially auspicious for reincarnation studies. At that time a past life insight can facilitate a major spiritual breakthrough.

FINANCE

Through June 11, Jupiter brightens your money sector. Look for ways to add to your earnings. Your Earth sign, the path to security in your birth chart, is Libra. This reminds you to be careful about how financial partnerships and other relationships affect your personal affluence. You'll find stability if you cultivate business relationships which allow you to be an individual and to innovate. The past two years, with serious Saturn in your Earth sign, have brought an awareness of how obligations to others have affected your spending power. The practical advice offered by others can be very helpful.

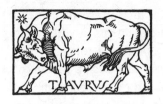

TAURUS
The year ahead for those
born under the sign of the Bull
April 20 – May 20

Slow, yet steady and stubborn, Taurus doesn't respond well to pressure and needs time to accept new ideas. Yet this luxury-loving sign, ruled by Venus, will almost always acquire what it needs to build a desirable lifestyle. An exquisite sensitivity to sound and an appreciation of color may manifest in musical talent or an aptitude for fashion and fine art.

The vernal equinox finds Venus and Jupiter, the most fortunate and benevolent planets, in Taurus. This extremely auspicious pattern continues until April 3. Devote Ostara rituals to financial goals, healing, or romance. Be alert to opportunity; your quality of life is definitely improving. A favorable grand trine in earth signs, formed with Pluto, Jupiter, and Mars, is an upbeat cycle that embraces you through June 11. Fulfilling obligations brings a sense of accomplishment. You'll discover inner reserves of strength. Reflect upon what you wish to cultivate. Just after the summer solstice, Venus completes a retrograde pattern in your 2nd house of finances. You can catch up on bills and may be offered a raise.

July and August find Mercury at a square to your Sun impacting home and family dynamics. At Lammastide, prepare a house blessing to dispel negative energies from your residence. Be patient, flexible, and diplomatic with argumentative relatives. A move or home improvement might be considered, but it's better to postpone a final decision until September 1.

The first two weeks of September, Mercury joins the Sun in Virgo, creating a positive aspect in your 5th house. Recreational travel and better communication with children can be expected. From the autumnal equinox through mid-October a stellium of planets, including Saturn, transits your health sector and makes a fateful quincunx aspect. It's a wonderful time to analyze factors affecting health situations, including past lives or family karma. Balance work with adequate rest and a wholesome diet.

On October 29 the Full Moon falls in your sign. Heed dreams and premonitions. Early November finds Mercury turning retrograde and joining Mars to create a stir in your 8th house of mysteries. A secret comes to light; it's a perfect time for investigations. Keep careful track of receipts and financial records. Be wary of business advice offered by others if it contradicts your better judgment. The lunar eclipse of November 28 promises the start of some changes regarding employment and earning ability. Be progressive and flexible. Situations linked to your security are in flux. Through December 25 Mars joins Pluto in Capricorn, creating favorable energies in your sector of philosophy and spirituality. Honor the Yuletide season with rituals for prosperity and growth.

January 1 – 19 ushers in an excellent Mercury transit. Focus on study, travel, and serious discussions or professional negotiations. Accept an offer to do a presentation or other public speaking. Finalize contracts and agreements. The outcome will be beneficial to you. January 20–Candlemas finds Venus prominent. It's a great time to experiment with fashion and beauty or to decorate your home or workplace.

February 3 – March 12: your 11th house is activated by several planets, including Mercury, Mars, and Neptune. Your goals are changing; so is your circle of friends. Check claims and credentials. Someone can be deceptive or misinformed. You might be drawn toward charitable endeavors. Offer a helping hand, but don't go beyond your comfort level. It's easy to be overly generous now and have regrets in weeks ahead. During winter's final days maintaining a peaceful and contemplative mood refreshes you.

HEALTH

Saturn completes a two-year passage through your health sector on October 5. Steady efforts to improve health early in the year should bring positive results by Samhain. The sign of Libra, which is associated with Eastern wisdom, has a special impact upon your health. Count calories and avoid sweets. A yoga sequence such as the Five Tibetans series of postures can help to enhance your strength and preserve your youth.

LOVE

May 16–June 28 finds Venus, the celestial love goddess, in retrograde motion. It's a perfect time to examine repeating patterns in relationships. During this retrograde the values and financial status of a loved one will be an important factor in determining whether a relationship works. October finds Venus blessing your 5th house of love. Woo someone by preparing a decorative table of autumn fruits and grains to share and burning a spicy incense. By Samhain the desired relationship should be secure.

SPIRITUALITY

Vulcan, a tiny cosmic body located between Mercury and the Sun, is your esoteric ruler. The axiom "I see and when the eye is opened all is illumined" suggests that study and the perfecting of skills are factors in realizing your spirituality. Neptune is impacted by supportive aspects in earth signs throughout May, promising tangible progress in spiritual awakening near your birthday. Have a solar return style horoscope prepared by your personal astrologer for greater clarity.

FINANCE

The eclipses this year affect your financial sectors. There may be changes in working conditions or sources of income. June and November will reveal the specifics. Jupiter, the luckiest of planets, is in your sign until mid-June. Finances have great potential in the spring; pursue opportunities to add to your savings then. Your Earth sign, the security source in your horoscope, is Scorpio. Recycle, improvise, and use what resources are on hand to preserve your assets.

GEMINI
The year ahead for those
born under the sign of the Twins
May 21–June 20

This restless, adaptable, Mercury-ruled sign is versatile, intellectual, and witty. Symbolized by the Twins, sometimes accused of being two-faced, Gemini is the zodiac's most dual personality. Natural teachers and promoters, they can be or do almost anything and adapt to any situation.

Spring's onset is a time to complete final chapters. Mercury is retrograde from the vernal equinox until April 5 in the 11th house of aspirations and associates. You might return to a past goal or former friends. Venus blesses you with a long passage through your sign April 4 – August 7, promising a cycle of great happiness. Your creative abilities and social contacts generate exceptional opportunities. Both romance and business are very promising.

May Eve finds Jupiter and the Sun hiding in your 12th house. It's a wonderful time to connect with nature. The first of two consecutive New Moons in Gemini, on May 20, is also a partial solar eclipse. Surprises and changes are coming. Late May through June is a very interesting time, with two eclipses coming up and a rare second New Moon in Gemini on June 19. Heed instincts; if a project arouses your enthusiasm,

follow it. On July 4 Mars changes signs, entering your 5th house of leisure, hobbies, and sports though the end of August. Your competitive energies are an asset. While Mercury is retrograde July 15 – August 9, reach out to help a troubled young person or an animal in need. Make sure vehicles are in good repair near Lammastide. Honor the Early Harvest by revisiting an old haunt. Your energy level is at a peak during the last half of August, enabling you to accomplish much.

September brings powerful mutable sign aspects to your Sun from several planets, including Jupiter and Neptune. Values are questioned. When in doubt trust your instincts. At the autumnal equinox check the validity of claims and credentials. Inflation, illusion, and a touch of deception are afoot. October 4 – 28 brings a beneficial transit to your home and family sector. Decorate or repair your dwelling. It's an ideal time to arrange a Feng Shui consultation or finalize real estate transactions.

From Samhain to November 16 Mars is in opposition. Your relationship sector is highlighted. Others have plans and ideas which impact you. Cope by considering all points of view. A legal matter may need attention. A lunar eclipse on November 28 conjoins your Sun, illuminating the specifics of patterns which began in the spring. As Yuletide nears, release that which no longer serves. Talkative, expressive companions provide you with valuable insights December 11 – 31.

Throughout January fiery, favorable influences from Mars and Jupiter offer travel opportunities and a variety of activity. A long cherished hope becomes a reality by Candlemas. February 2 – 25: Venus dances through a benevolent trine to Jupiter, drawing your Sun into the mix. A spiritual healing circle, yoga class, or meditation group is rewarding. Near Valentine's Day, in-law and grandparent-grandchild relationships touch your heart joyfully.

Retrograde Mercury joins Neptune, Mars, and the Sun in your career sector as March begins. Things are intense and hidden work factors are about to come to light. Good or bad, all is not as it seems. The New Moon on March 11 brings the specifics into focus. Don't make a hasty decision and walk out on a project March 1 – 12. Winter's final days are best devoted to tying up loose ends. Something or someone leaves your professional environment. Have faith that everything happens for a reason.

HEALTH

Your birthday month brings the blessing of improved health. Jupiter, the celestial healer, enters your sign on June 12 where it remains through the year. It's a perfect time to implement new wellness programs. April, September, and the late winter reveal some challenging aspects in the mutable signs, bringing health concerns linked to stress. A short break when everything seems overwhelming can make a huge difference in how you feel physically and mentally.

LOVE

The June 4 lunar eclipse makes a splash in your 7th house of partnerships. Your relationship status might change or an established bond can move to a new level. Venus makes an exceptionally long passage through your sign from early April – early August. This is a very upbeat influence for love and intimacy with the one you cherish. While Venus is retrograde from May 16 – June 28 an old flame could rekindle or you'll have an improved perspective concerning a lost love.

SPIRITUALITY

Venus is the esoteric and spiritual ruler of Gemini. The spring and summer sabbats this year find Venus hovering near your Sun. It's an exceptional cycle for spiritual awakening. The eclipses of May 20 and November 28 are ideal for magical workings involving personal development. "I recognize my other self and in the waning of that self I grow and glow" is your phrase for spiritual reflection. It encourages nourishing only the good, constructive, and compassionate Twin, not the negative one. Humor is helpful in this quest.

FINANCE

Your pot of gold at the end of the prosperity rainbow is reached through following your Earth sign of Sagittarius. Always direct exploration toward a purpose you truly believe in. Good sportsmanship, a healthy competitive spirit, continuing education, and the healing support of animal companions can all be a part of your path to acquiring financial acumen. This year May, January, and February hold your best financial opportunities.

CANCER
The year ahead for those
born under the sign of the Crab
June 21–July 22

Life's issues are met indirectly by the side-stepping celestial Crab. Cancers are guided by an interior ocean of ebbing and flowing emotional waves. Sensitive, subjective Moon children absorb the essence of their surroundings; therefore, they must associate with only the upbeat or their welfare can be jeopardized. Cancer cherishes the safe havens of heritage and home.

Honor the blessing of friendship as spring begins. From the vernal equinox through All Fool's Day, Venus brightens your 11th house with a supportive sextile aspect. Past favors you've offered are returned. Casual acquaintances you assist now become closer, valuable contacts in the year ahead. During April and May, the Sun and Jupiter reinforce the benefits of networking. At Beltane, bless keepsakes to offer to your closest friends. June 8 – 25: Mercury races through Cancer. Address transportation needs. The path is prepared for acquiring your dream vehicle. Travel or planning upcoming journeys is favored too. Devote magical workings at the summer solstice to travel, contracts, and communication concerns to quickly and profitably conclude meetings and negotiations.

During July and August Mars joins Saturn in your sector of home and property. A residence or workplace could require repair. Expect some challenges involving obligations to the very elderly or very young. Patience and cheerfulness are essential. Issues arise which can take time to resolve. The New Moon on July 19 favors a new approach to coping with an ongoing situation. Lammastide is ideal for performing a house blessing. The positive effects of this ceremony will manifest between August 8 – September 6 when Venus glides through Cancer in a harmonious aspect to Neptune. This planetary pattern demonstrates the healing ability of true love combined with faith. Answers to a dilemma can come through a dream.

From just before the autumnal equinox through October 6 Mars empowers you through the 5th house of romance, art, and pleasure. Invest effort in strengthening a love relationship or in creative projects. Life is joyful, and vitality peaks. During the last three weeks of October Saturn changes signs and trines Neptune, activating your 9th house. This is a highly mystical and spiritual influence. As All Hallows nears, messages from loved ones who have passed offer solace. Meditation awakens your psychic aptitudes and provides deeper insight into previously puzzling situations. Other cultures or travel to another part of the world is appealing. Also, you could perfect the art of astral projection and take a journey that way. The total solar eclipse of November 13 brings the importance of this pattern into focus. It also ushers in a cycle of great creativity. Express an original idea; rewards will come.

Mid-November through the winter solstice: Mars and Pluto move in opposition to you. Relationships are a focus. Others are competitive and intense. Expectations are voiced. Tolerate anger or demands with quiet good humor, but back away from really difficult individuals. Dedicate a Yuletide ceremony to peace. The December 28 Full Moon in Cancer inaugurates a four-week cycle during which you'll accomplish things promptly. During January, a good affirmation is "there's no time like the present." Legal and ethical issues require attention as Candlemas nears.

From February 6 through winter's end, Mercury is in your sister water sign, Pisces. Your heart and head form an unbeatable combination for study and problem solving. At February's end, a highly sensitive and idealistic Venusian influence develops, remaining in force during the first three weeks of March. Unconditional love prevails. You'll be pleased with the direction a close relationship takes.

HEALTH

The June 4 eclipse affects your health sector. Heed your body's signals. June is a good time to overcome counterproductive health patterns. An animal companion can play an important part in healing. Pressures related to professional aspirations or a partnership must be kept under control. A tight square between Uranus and Pluto affects your 10th and 7th houses all year. Keep your work environment and closest commitments wholesome. Early in October,

when Saturn changes signs, your vitality should improve.

LOVE

A strong earth sign influence in spring favors a sincere, supportive approach to love. Above all, be a best friend to those you care for. Venus is in your sign the last three weeks of August, promising deepening romantic happiness. Prepare a love token featuring the number thirteen to direct the magic of November 13's total solar eclipse toward blessing your desired relationship. That eclipse is in your love sector.

SPIRITUALITY

Esoteric astrology assigns Neptune as your spiritual ruler. This mystical planet is in the midst of an extended passage through Pisces, your 9th house, also the area where the August 31 Blue Moon falls. The lunation should mark a brilliant month, taking spiritual awakening to a new level. "I build a lighted house and therein dwell" is your spiritual mission statement, hinting that creating a metaphysical atmosphere at home, perhaps a dedicated altar or meditation area, is helpful.

FINANCE

As spring begins, two strong financial indicators, Jupiter and Venus, square your 2nd house of money. Live within your means. Finances should improve by late autumn. Don't let anyone override your better financial judgment. Be wary of advice regarding money. Don't assume the fiscal responsibilities of another. March and December promise stellar financial opportunities.

LEO
The year ahead for those
born under the sign of the Lion
July 23–August 22

Self-reliant and magnanimous, the Lion cuts a flamboyant figure while striding through the jungle of life. Determined, warm-hearted, and generous, this fire sign is secretly a playful kitten at heart. You meet life with a royal flair, blending business and responsibility with love and pleasure.

Early spring finds Venus tagging Jupiter on your midheaven, the point of highest recognition and aspirations. Be aware of new trends in your profession. Networking with business associates is enjoyable and financially advantageous as All Fool's Day passes. April 17 – May 9: Mercury joins Uranus in your 9th house of education and journeys. Plan to travel or enroll in classes. It's a perfect time to study foreign languages or master secret codes and cryptograms.

Mars remains in your 2nd house of finances until July 3. Your desire to have the best, both for yourself and loved ones, generates a struggle for greater material security. Keep a sense of balance regarding values though. During the spring and early summer enjoy what you have. If the financial situation grows too stressful, a little patience will improve the situation.

At the May 20 eclipse a stellium of planets begins to form in your 11th house, an influence in effect through the summer solstice. You'll be inspired by talented and interesting friends. Become active in an organization you find worthwhile. Suddenly old goals fade and new aspirations develop. Mercury transits Leo from June 26 – August 31 promising a summer of travel, interesting discussions, and sharpened intellectual prowess. As the sun sets on the day of the New Moon in Leo, August 17, focus on where you are in your life and what goals you'd like to reach before next year's birthday.

September 7 – October 3 Venus delivers your heart's desire. This is a most promising romantic and artistic trend. Do magical workings to facilitate a balance between the head and heart. Mid-October through November 16 Mars energizes you, making a benevolent trine aspect. The element fire is prominent. At All Hallows emphasize the mystique of flames. The total solar eclipse on November 13 profoundly impacts your residence and family situation. It might be time for a move. Relatives have a few surprises up their sleeves. Maintain your home as November ends; your dwelling needs blessings, love, and care.

Early to mid-December: Mercury, Venus, and the Sun brighten your 5th house. A child is a source of delight; love situations are upbeat; there is time to pursue a favorite pastime. At the winter solstice, add frankincense and myrrh to the burning Yule log and request an awakening of your highest potentials. January finds Mars in opposition. Companions are competitive and outspoken. Cooperation is a must. The Leo Full Moon on January 26 returns your power. Influential people notice and appreciate you.

A partner displays charm and true talent February 2 – 25 while Venus accents your 7th house. Be supportive. You could meet a very attractive, gifted person during the week of the New Moon on February 10. March begins on a note of intrigue. Water sign transits, including Neptune, Mars, and the Sun, affect your 8th house. Others have financial strategies which can impact your security. An estate or inheritance might be involved. It's worthwhile to do research. This is also a wonderful time to attend a séance. The gates to the afterlife are unlocked.

HEALTH

Saturn, ruler of your health sector, is retrograde until June 26. Patience is the key to wellness during this entire time. Work toward fitness goals gradually. Allow your body time to heal. If possible, delay any elective or radical medical procedures until the Sun is well aspected in fire signs and thus favorable for health matters August 10 – 22 and again December 1 – 19. Carry a heart-shaped talisman to protect your health and longevity. Leo has a traditional link to the heart.

LOVE

The focus of your affections and the very meaning of true love are in transition, caused by the June 4 lunar eclipse in your sector of romance. Venus retrograde in May and June opposes the eclipse point and can generate complications. Keep your commitment status the same during the spring; allow love to evolve as it will. Grant the one you love enough freedom. Love links brighten in late summer and early autumn as well as mid-December through early January when Venus is in harmony.

SPIRITUALITY

The Sun is both the familiar exoteric and the esoteric or spiritual ruler of this sign. The increased sunspot and solar flare activity anticipated can be important regarding your spiritual awakening. The starts of each new season are your spiritual turning points. That's when the Sun's influence shifts. There is balance at the vernal and autumnal equinoxes, while the solstices accent the importance of rest and darkness. "Measure well the bright hours, for the dark hours pass unmarked" is your spiritual mission statement.

FINANCE

Being detail-oriented and organized in money matters serves you well. Meticulous Virgo rules your 2nd house of earnings. A healthy working environment strengthens financial dividends. Finances look encouraging in September, February, and March. Fanciful Neptune influences play with your security structure this year. A dream, inspiration, or interesting financial offer is worthy of consideration, but think things through. Don't take dangerous risks or act on impulse.

VIRGO
The year ahead for those
born under the sign of the Virgin
August 23-September 22

Industrious, meticulous, and earthy Virgo is an excellent manager. Ruled by Mercury, guardian of the intellect, you're respected for being clearheaded and detail-oriented. Conscientious, with a natural fascination for health topics, Virgos find service brings deep rewards. The celestial Grain Gatherer is critical of imperfection and might have a sharp tongue, yet dislikes displays of anger.

Spring begins with a pensive "same old, same old" mood. Retrograde Mercury backslides over the cusp of your 7th and 8th houses to oppose your Sun. This aspect remains until April 16. Closest relationships repeat predictable patterns. Support what is good about the old times, but discard that which has become stale. It's a wonderful energy for experiencing a past life regression. Insight into a previous incarnation may help to make the best of present circumstances.

On April 21 the New Moon in Taurus accents a grand trine in earth signs. Practical considerations are a focus. Your energy level and motivation peak. A sense of strength and confidence propels you through the next several weeks. From May 10 – June 11 Taurus transits,

including the Sun, Mercury, and Jupiter highlight your 9th house. Travel is both enlightening and profitable. It's a great time to make choices and finalize contracts. The June 4 eclipse affects home and family. A decision can be made about living arrangements. A new attitude about what family truly means emerges. As the summer solstice nears, your career sector is active. Opportunities to profit from your professional skills emerge. Let others see what you can do. Assume new duties or consider starting an ambitious project you've longed to try.

During July and August Mars joins Saturn in your 2nd house of finances. You'll be focused on resolving security issues. Be guided by the traditional work ethic and patiently keep trying. A breakthrough comes just as Mercury enters your sign on September 1. Your birthday month favors a journey. The New Moon on September 15 brings insight concerning which theme you'd do well to follow during the year to come. At the autumnal equinox others seek your counsel. Autumn's most colorful days coincide with a joyful cycle regarding romance, as Venus blesses your sign October 4 – 28.

As November begins you'll juggle career and domestic issues while mutable sign planets agitate the angles of your birth chart. Make a list of priorities. The November 13 solar eclipse in your 3rd house brings a burst of mental energy coupled with needed information. You'll figure out how to restore balance as the Yuletide season approaches. Mid-November through the winter solstice brings a potent

Mars influence highlighting your sector of love, recreation, and creativity. Issue and accept invitations. The good times continue through January; both Mercury and Venus favorably accent romance and leisure and stimulate creative ideas. The deep winter is warmed by good companions and enjoyable pursuits. Improved finances are part of the pleasure.

Candlemas brings an abrupt shift in focus. There's a planetary stir in your health sector. Surround the Imbolc altar with a circle of medicinal herbs and light reiki-charged healing candles. During March your sector of commitment is accented. The importance of cooperation becomes apparent. Psychic and spiritual links to others are a vital part of your life as winter wanes. Questions of integrity and competitive feelings might surface. March 1 – 7 brings a strong Venus–Saturn influence. Both formal regulations and the unwritten rules of good etiquette should be heeded. Tensions with others ease after Mars changes signs on March 12.

HEALTH

Uranus, ruler of your 6th house, is the health indicator in your birth chart. Innovative and highly technical health care procedures fascinate you. Uranus is in the midst of a long passage through Aries now, making you especially progressive in maintaining wellness. The effects of stress, of taking on too much work, can take a toll on your health from Ostara until July 3 while Mars is in your sign. Pace yourself, and your health will greatly improve by summer's end.

LOVE

The Full Moon on July 3 conjoins Pluto in your 5th house of romance. The following four weeks can be intense in the love arena. Put the beloved's wishes first, even if it means letting go. The Blue Moon of August 31 activates your 7th house of committed partnerships. Insight into strong bonds with others, deepening loyalties, and maybe a promising new relationship can be expected during the next eight weeks.

SPIRITUALITY

Esoteric astrology offers the Moon as your spiritual ruler. The monthly pattern of lunar phases and signs facilitates deeper spiritual awareness. Invoke a favorite moon goddess as a spiritual guide. Madonna images of all traditions speak to the higher spiritual influence of your sign. Explore your spiritual mission further as you reflect upon the statement "Both Mother and Child, I Am, I Matter." The February 25 Full Moon is in Virgo. Reflect upon it to assure spiritual realization.

FINANCE

From the vernal equinox until October 6 serious Saturn sits in your financial sector. There might be some old monetary obligations to meet. Patient planning is essential during the spring and summer. Your Earth sign of security is Pisces. Charity and sacrifice link to your financial planning. Give only what you can comfortably afford to spare. Do not ever allow others to drain your resources. The financial outlook is bright in January. Debts can be resolved then and extra funds may be available.

LIBRA
The year ahead for those
born under the sign of the Scales
September 23–October 23

The Scale finds its perfect balance while weighing honor and justice. This Venus-ruled sign appreciates beauty and companionship, always placing love first. An aversion to disharmony leads to the development of excellent social and negotiation skills. Adroitly meeting one situation after another, Libra appears to vacillate but actually is considering all sides of the issue.

Greet the spring with a huge sigh of relief. Saturn is retrograde in the final decanate of a long passage through your sign. The past year and a half has brought some challenges, but you'll enjoy a bit of a respite until June 26 when Saturn will be direct again. On April 6 the Full Moon brightens your sign. Others welcome your ideas enthusiastically during the four weeks following the lunation. Mid-April through Beltane finds Mercury touching base with Uranus in your 7th house. Companions make surprise announcements. Your superb negotiation skills serve you well and help you maintain peace. Appreciate an eccentric person.

On May 25 Mercury joins Venus and the Sun in your 9th house. An excellent cycle for travel begins. The eclipse of June 4 promises exposure to new ideas and interests. However, a volatile situation with a neighbor or in-law might have to be addressed simultaneously. From mid-June through the summer solstice there is much going on beneath the surface. Mars is buried in your 12th house until July 3, indicating that there's some anger to release. It's essential not to underestimate or annoy an adversary. The New Moon on July 19 is in your 10th house of career goals. This lunation strongly aspects both Mars and Saturn in your 1st house. Much is demanded of you, but great rewards can come if you're willing to work hard. August 9–September 6 Venus glides over your midheaven, easing pressures you've been under. Professional recognition draws nearer, and the workload lightens during the weeks before the autumnal equinox.

September 17 – October 5: Mercury dashes through Libra bringing insight and understanding. Pursue travel opportunities near your birthday; a change of scene brings unexpected rewards. At the New Moon in Libra on October 15, Saturn finally moves out of your sign. A duty which has weighed heavily for about the past two years miraculously evaporates or is suddenly much easier to manage. Lightheartedness abounds as you prepare for All Hallows. Host or attend an extravagant party. Venus enters Libra on October 29, remaining until November 21. Cherished wishes materialize. The lunar eclipse on November 28 impacts your 9th house and is highly spiritual. Walk a labyrinth or visit a sacred site.

Through December your home and family sector is strongly affected by

Mars, Pluto, and, at the solstice, the Sun. Communicate with family members about holiday plans. Make sure the expectations you have are agreeable to all. A quiet Yuletide observance might be best. January brings you a great energy surge as Mars makes a favorable trine to your Sun until February 1. Look into exercise programs in early 2013. Creative projects and hobbies would enrich your life too.

At Candlemas love stars brighten, for Venus enters your romance and pleasure sector where it remains until February 25. The New Moon on February 10 brings a sense of security concerning love. In March several planets, including Mercury and Neptune, highlight your 6th house, which relates to animal companions. Psychic links to pets strengthen as winter ends. A favorite familiar could display healing aptitudes. Follow that first impression if you encounter a new animal who wants to join your household.

HEALTH

Karmic or hard-to-diagnose situations often play a role in your physical well-being. Elusive Neptune rules your health sector. Faith is always a factor in your ability to overcome health challenges. The Blue Moon on August 31 activates your wellness indicators. The four-week period following that date is a wonderful time for seeking relief from medical conditions. In October, when Saturn leaves your sign, your overall health and vitality improve.

LOVE

Firm friendship is often the beginning of a successful love bond, for the humanitarian sign of Aquarius rules your 5th house of romance. Business networking, community service, and political organizations can pave the way for a lasting relationship. While Venus is retrograde from May 16 – June 28 don't change your relationship status. Love can get complicated then; humor and tolerance are musts. Late October through mid-November and the month of February are very promising times to find romantic happiness.

SPIRITUALITY

Persephone, a trans-Pluto satellite, is your esoteric ruler. Forgiveness and knowing when to leave counterproductive situations at opportune times play a part in your spiritual growth. "I choose the way between two great lines of force" is a spiritual mission statement to reflect upon. The eclipses of May 20 and November 28 fall in your sector of philosophical beliefs, indicating times of spiritual awakening.

FINANCE

Your Earth sign is Aries; your route to wealth is the adventurous warrior path. This favors establishing a financial identity independent of close relationships. Developing salable job skills, exploration, innovation, and competition without combativeness help you achieve security. In autumn, Saturn enters your money sector in favorable mutual reception with Pluto in Capricorn. Your values and financial goals are about to shift. Hard work is involved, but there's a very promising money situation overall as the year ends.

SCORPIO

The year ahead for those
born under the sign of the Scorpion
October 24–November 21

Swept along in a torrent of strong likes and dislikes, an aura of reserved dignity envelops Scorpios. A touch of secrecy is pervasive, adding to the charisma and intrigue which create a magnetic personality. You delve beneath the surface with deep sensitivity. This contributes to your impressive survival and problem-solving skills.

Spring begins with Venus brightening your relationship sector. Partners are supportive. Through All Fool's Day it's easy to be a team player. An especially thoughtful, talented person will be attentive. Even if this is a tad annoying, show appreciation with a heartfelt expression of thanks. If you're not interested in an intimate relationship though, be sure to gently let your feelings be known. On April 11 Pluto, your ruler, turns retrograde until mid-September. Your 3rd house is affected, so transportation arrangements might have to be changed. Have an alternative in place if a conveyance is at all unreliable. You'll also be receiving information which tempts you to change some long-held opinions.

Near the Scorpio Full Moon on May 5 your emotional energy peaks. Feelings spill over, eliciting reactions from others. Direct your focus constructively and the world will be at your feet. A message from the spirit realm is likely. The last half of May finds Mercury and Jupiter in opposition to you. Be patient if others are slow to cooperate; there might be a good reason for this. Flexibility on your part will help in reaching goals. On June 8 Mercury enters your sister water sign of Cancer and favorably aspects Neptune. Through the summer solstice travel is very favorable. It's also a great cycle for creative writing. If you've always wanted to write for publication, now is the time. Your efforts could result in a successful book, maybe illustrated with your own photographs or drawings.

Finances are the focus as July begins. Mars enters your 2nd house of income and possessions where it makes a powerful conjunction with Saturn in mid-August. Hard work is essential, but your efforts will be rewarded by the autumnal equinox. During September your natural tendency toward secrecy is more pronounced than ever. A 12th house influence brings enjoyment through peace and quiet.

From September through early October, release grudges and anger. Much can be accomplished when you aren't hampered by negative feelings. On October 6 a positive Mercury influence develops, making it easier to keep a cool head and find solutions. The last three weeks of October are wonderful for writing, study, travel, and public speaking. Saturn moves forward at the same time, entering your sign for the next two years. There's a supportive mutual reception between Saturn and Pluto. A sense of rebirth prevails; you're on the brink of a promising new phase of life. At All Hallows recognize that deaths are merely new beginnings. The total solar eclipse in your sign on November 13 further accents both fare-wells and greetings.

November 15 – December 10 favors study and travel, for Mercury will be active again. You'll become reflective and serious near Thanksgiving, but by Yuletide you'll welcome a bit of debate and controversy. A stimulating exchange of ideas is promised by several 3rd house transits. Juggling several projects will stave off ennui.

January opens with domestic issues needing attention. Home maintenance can be involved. A neighbor or sibling appreciates kind words. Family dynamics become less complex during February. February 2 – March 12 an upbeat Mars aspect supports creative expression and sports. There's time to enjoy yourself. Winter's last days offer a romantic interlude, as Venus brightens your love sector. A gesture of tender affection from an admirer tugs at your heart strings.

HEALTH

March 22, the New Moon activates your health sector. Spring's earliest days are wonderful for cleansing toxins: consider a tonic of apple cider vinegar mixed with raw honey and purified water. Meditate to attune to your body's signals. Address any minor health issues at Ostara. That way, when the November 13 eclipse ushers in new activities, you'll be in optimum physical shape.

LOVE

Neptune stays in your love sector all year, facilitating telepathic exchanges with those you love. Intimate bonds have an ethereal fragility, a karmic or mystical feel. Don't let love be blind though: maintain realistic expectations concerning intimate relationships. Dreams offer guidance about love's perplexities. August 8 – September 6, November 22 – December 15, and February 26 through winter's end are times when Venus smiles on you and love triumphs.

SPIRITUALITY

Your spiritual and esoteric astrology ruler is Mars, promising some struggles as you explore the spiritual path. "Warrior am I and from the battle I emerge triumphant" is your spiritual mission statement. The message is that overcoming various obstacles will hone spiritual awareness. Begin by seeing all adversaries as teachers in disguise. Mars brings a dose of spiritual fire your way late August through early October when it conjoins your Sun.

FINANCE

Neptune stays in your love sector all year, facilitating telepathy with loved ones. Intimate bonds have an ethereal fragility – a karmic or mystical feel – but don't let love be blind. Maintain realistic expectations. Dreams offer romantic guidance. August 8 – September 6, November 22 – December 15, and February 26 through winter's end are times when Venus smiles on you and love triumphs.

SAGITTARIUS

The year ahead for those
born under the sign of the Archer
November 22–December 21

Outspoken and self-reliant, the Centaur possesses generosity and an independent spirit. Challenges motivate you to win and persevere, while curiosity leads you to explore. Hence faraway places and foreign-born companions often shape your destiny. Animals, particularly horses and canines, are dear to your heart. Competitions and sporting events can be a part of this bond.

Early spring finds Mercury retrograde in your home and family sector. A recent move might have been unsettling. An ongoing situation needs attention, possibly a repair or remodeling project. April 5–16 offers a way to resolve disputes. Mid-April through May Day finds mutable sign planets in aspect to Mars. There's a great deal of excitement related to your career, but undercurrents of anger and stress are present. A sense of humor helps if a competitor seems to be getting the best of you. By May 9 a Mercury-Uranus aspect comes to the rescue. Your originality enables you to rise above the undesirable. During the remainder of May, your 6th house of wellness is strong.

The lunar eclipse of June 4 is in your sign. This commences a time of new beginnings and unleashed potential. Retrograde Venus encourages you to reevaluate partnerships of all kinds through June 28. Legal situations improve during July, when Jupiter joins Venus in your 7th house. Expect a complete turnaround regarding problem people by Lammastide; a former adversary becomes a supporter.

Throughout August, Mercury dashes through Leo, supported by the Sun and Uranus: a beneficial time to examine philosophical concepts or plan a pilgrimage. You can be both a good student and a teacher. During September, Mars slips into your 12th house of hidden things. Turbulence lurks beneath the surface until early October. Research uncovers surprises; it's essential to be honest with yourself. A quiet act of assistance to one in need is fine, but only if charity isn't misplaced and doesn't drain resources too much.

The weeks before Samhain find your energy level high. Your 1st and 11th houses are prominent, activated by influences from Mars and the Sun. This can be a time of major progress.

Pace yourself in physically demanding activities. If impatience arises, focus on problem resolution: don't give way to anger. Your social circle has greater impact on your life than usual. Cultivate nurturing friendships. During November and December, Mercury retrogrades back and forth into your sign, punctuated by two eclipses. Specific plans are subject to change, but the approach of Yuletide finds you traveling and enthused. An old obligation is completed. Animal companions sense that something is afoot. Heed their efforts to communicate with you.

On December 14, Uranus turns direct in your 5th house of pleasure and romance. Two days later, Venus waltzes into Sagittarius: revel in the warmth and happiness through January 8. Finances are promising, too. From mid-January through Candlemas, your 3rd house sets the pace. Short journeys, outings, and errands keep you busy. News coverage reveals essential information. February brings a gathering of planets in your home and family sector with unconditional love binding family members. An unspoken agreement brings peace. February 7-8 and 19-22 and again at the New Moon on March 11: Neptunian nuances heighten sensitivity, favorably influencing home and family. March 12–20 brings a welcome change of pace with a fiery, progressive Mars-Uranus conjunction in Aries. You'll revel in a sense of newfound freedom. Romance and creative projects blossom.

HEALTH

From the vernal equinox through June 11 your health is blessed by Jupiter in your sector of wellness. It's a great time to take care of health checkups and set new health-related goals. The Sagittarius eclipse of June 4 brings a renewed sensitivity to your physical self. Heed hunches concerning your health during the springtime. While Jupiter is retrograde from early October–late January don't be a couch potato. A lapse into counterproductive habits, such as the wrong diet or lack of exercise, could bring consequences.

LOVE

Two eclipses, on May 20 and November 28, create a splash in your 7th house of relationships. The impact lasts all year. April 4–August 7 Venus makes a long passage through your partnership sector. You'll have an active social life with much loving attention coming your way. Explore your feelings concerning commitment. Delay hasty changes in your relationship status if there is any doubt. Mid-December through early January ushers in a very positive Venus transit. From your birthday month through Twelfth Night, happiness in love is promised.

SPIRITUALITY

"I see the goal, I reach the goal and see another" is the mission statement of the Earth, your ruler in spiritual astrology. Accepting the circumstances of your birth philosophically and seeing the good in your immediate surroundings assures spiritual progress. Connecting with plants, animals, and places of scenic beauty are key factors. The New Moon on December 13 favors spiritual reflection and progress.

FINANCE

You can successfully blend spiritual with financial values, because your spiritual ruler, the Earth, also is your link to monetary security. Your Earth sign is versatile Gemini. Being a jack-of-all-trades serves you well. Upgrade your earning ability with study. Communication skills are paramount in fulfilling your material desires. Late winter is the most profitable time during the year to come, as your lucky star, Jupiter, will be in direct motion and moving rapidly after Candlemas.

CAPRICORN
The year ahead for those
born under the sign of the Goat
December 22–January 19

Quietly serious and ambitious, The Goat steps carefully climbing life's mountains while calculating the best path to success. With a healthy regard for conventions and traditional customs, Capricorn combines the best traits of the ambassador with the scientist. Ruled by solemn Saturn, there is a stately and reserved quality about the very young Goat. This changes to a good humored exuberance as time passes.

Spring finds you full of happiness. Venus, Jupiter, Mars, and Pluto glide harmoniously in a grand earth trine. These good times last through the summer solstice. Venus is especially supportive from March 20 – April 3: pursue true love. April 4 – May Eve is excellent for improving relations with in-laws or for outings with grandparents and grandchildren. May 10 – 24: Mercury joins the mix of good earth energy, with a focus on your 5th house. It's an optimum time for vacation travel and serious conversation with loved ones. Jot down creative ideas that come your way during this time. A brainstorming session with a colleague can pay off.

June finds the Sun and retrograde Venus in your health sector. Be sensitive concerning how diet and beverages affect your well-being. It's easy to overindulge and binge if you're not careful. A new animal companion may join your household, offering love and loyalty near the summer solstice. The Full Moon in your sign on July 3 is powerfully linked to Pluto. You'll be intensely aware of changing economic and social trends in the world throughout July. Political unrest and weather conditions motivate you to make preparations to provide for the future.

Devote Lammastide observances to a blessing for your career path. August finds both Mars and Saturn near your midheaven, powerfully impacting professional situations and status. Work hard and patiently do your best. Face challenges gallantly. September 1 – 16 Mercury races into Virgo and comes to the rescue in your 9th house. Important information comes to light which has an upbeat bearing on your reputation and professional situation. Business travel and meetings can be very productive; extra study pays off. By All Hallows the difficult situation should be a mere memory. Saturn changes signs in October, beginning a two-year passage through your 11th house while in a mutual reception with Pluto in Capricorn in your 1st house. This unique pattern brings new goals and opportunities your way, but much will be expected of you. While Mars is in your sign from November 17 – December 25 keep a lid on anger and impatience; keep moving forward.

Early January brings ability to cope with stress and solve dilemmas as Mercury conjoins your Sun. Your competence reaches a new level. Venus in

Capricorn brightens your life from January 9 – February 1. Your birthday and the weeks to follow promise love and happiness. Acquaintances are especially kind during the week of January 11, which marks the New Moon in your sign. This New Moon is very favorable for arranging priorities.

Candlemas brings focus to your financial sector with the urge to make purchases and increase earnings. Remember to want what you already have, be who you are, and do what you can — while living within your means. Saturn goes retrograde on February 19, which can temporarily delay your progress. An issue thought to be resolved may need tweaking. In March, water sign transits make friendly sextile aspects in your 3rd and 11th houses, favoring data gathering and greater involvement with worthwhile organizations. February 24 – March 18: verify appointments and directions and allow extra time for your daily commute while Mercury is retrograde.

HEALTH
Two Gemini eclipses on May 20 and November 28 highlight your 6th house of health, forming a quincunx, the aspect of fate, to your Sun. Alternative treatments for health conditions can be appealing now, but investigate them thoroughly before using. Eclipses always bring changes; it's essential to remain aware that your health is in flux and make adjustments accordingly. Work on your flexibility and circulation. Massage, yoga, and stretching exercises can be most helpful.

LOVE
The most benevolent of planets, Venus and Jupiter, brighten your love sector during the spring. Express your deepest feelings. Since Taurus, sign of the gardener, is involved in the favorable transits, offer a bouquet of flowers, perhaps a traditional tussie mussie, at Beltane. Include a card which describes the symbolism of the carefully selected blooms. By June 11 either a commitment is finalized with your new love or an existing bond will strengthen.

SPIRITUALITY
Saturn, planet of discipline and boundaries, is your esoteric spiritual ruler as well as your traditional ruler. Saturn enters Scorpio in October, beginning a two-year mutual reception with mysterious Pluto: tremendous spiritual potential begin to unfold. All Hallows promises to be profoundly spiritual. "Lost am I in light supernal" is your spiritual mission statement, revealing that worldly goods are lost in the transcendent value of spiritual illumination.

FINANCE
Uranus rules your financial sector, making you inherently savvy when it comes to money management and acquiring profitable job skills. Observe emerging global financial trends to help plan ahead near the July 3 Full Moon in Capricorn. This entire year finds Uranus in your 4th house. A family business, real estate transactions, or the buying and selling of collectibles can impact finances favorably. Early spring and late autumn mark the most profitable times.

AQUARIUS
The year ahead for those
born under the sign of the Water Bearer
January 20–February 18

Personable and amiable, Aquarius is the best friend of the zodiac and usually gets along well with almost everyone. The Water Bearer's pitcher overflows. Resources, especially advice, are generously shared with all of humanity. Still, you secretly suffer if you encounter rejection or unkindness and will withdraw once disenchanted by another. An inventive truth seeker, gadgets and progressive ideas fascinate you.

Interior decorating, including a good spring cleaning, is your focus at the vernal equinox as Jupiter draws attention to your home and family sector. Spaciousness and comfort are priorities. An addition to your home or perhaps a new dwelling may be on your agenda by Mother's Day. Your own need to mother or be mothered is a focus through May. The eclipse of May 20 is highlighted by a favorable Venus-Saturn trine impacting your 5th house. Romantic liaisons create joy during the weeks before Midsummer's Day. Late May through June is a highly inspirational cycle overall. A hobby, sport, or artistic pursuit can be the impetus.

On June 26 Mercury begins a long passage through your 7th house where it forms an opposition aspect. Partners are talkative, but might not always agree with you. Negotiation and compromise are essential. This need for communication peaks at the Full Moon in your sign on August 1. Legal matters can be time-consuming during August. Relegate disputes, including court dates, to the back burner of your life. The Blue Moon on August 31 brings new perspectives. Progress can be made toward a resolution in early September.

September 7 – October 3 Venus follows on the heels of Mercury. Goodwill builds, and someone you're committed to is more content. Plan a ritual honoring loyalty and love at the autumnal equinox. In October fixed sign planets impact your 10th house of fame and fortune. Respect the status quo; don't pressure professional associates if they're reluctant to make changes. There can be undercurrents of unrest or competitive feelings. Relieve stress and generate some smiles by decorating your workplace for Halloween. Suggest a costume contest to coworkers, then surprise everyone by presenting small prizes to all, whether they participated in the fun or not. Harmony will be restored.

During the first three weeks of November Venus is in Libra overseeing a wonderful air sign influence in your 9th house. Friendships deepen with those of a different cultural background. The total eclipse on November 13 profoundly impacts your professional situation. Be receptive to a transfer or other changes. A coworker seeks greener pastures. As the winter solstice approaches, several planets accent your 11th house of hopes and wishes. The New Moon on December 13 reveals the specifics. It's very important to go within and decide what you want. Waste no time or mental energy on dead issues. At Yule bless your long-term goals by visualizing light around each one while the Yule log burns.

January brings energy and initiative, for Mars adds fire to your life by transiting your sign all month long. Release anger or resentment. Instead, smile and remember that success is the best revenge. Activity refreshes you. Travel prospects, possibly for a ski trip, are excellent January 20 – February 5. By February 1 Jupiter completes its retrograde in your love sector and Venus glides toward Aquarius. You'll feel more confident about the best direction to go with a romantic involvement. Near your birthday the accomplishments of a younger family member or friend bring joy. February 10's New Moon in your sign emphasizes the future and growth.

March opens with practical considerations. Several planets, including retrograde Mercury, gather in your sector of finances. Keep receipts and balance the budget. On March 13, Mars moves out of the mix. Tension involving money lessens during winter's final days.

HEALTH

Drink plenty of fresh water, juice, and tea to cleanse your system of toxins and help maintain a healthy weight. July 14 – December 14 your ruling planet, Uranus, is retrograde. During that five-month period don't relapse into negative health habits. The Full Moon on December 28 in your 6th house of health favorably aspects Neptune. Faith healing, home remedies, or alternative medicines can be helpful during the four weeks following that lunation.

LOVE

Jupiter enters your 5th house of love on June 12 and remains there through the end of winter, exuding joy and blessings. Your prospects for finding happiness this year are wonderful if you remember that your celestial benefactor, Jupiter, is the planet of growth and new horizons. Keep your options open and maintain a broad outlook as you await the arrival of your own Love Boat. Swim out to welcome it in July, early November, or February.

SPIRITUALITY

Jupiter is the esoteric spiritual ruler of Aquarius, indicating that an expansive, liberal interpretation of traditional philosophical teachings will help you to awaken spiritually. Foreign travel and exploring the beliefs of other cultures are your spiritual guidelines. "Water of life am I, poured forth for thirsty people" is your spiritual mission statement. This suggests that sharing spiritual teachings for the benefit of humanity as a whole will encourage your personal spiritual practices to evolve.

FINANCE

Dreamy, elusive Neptune holds sway over your financial sector. Secrecy and discretion protects your wealth. As you fall asleep, ask for financial guidance from your dreams. Record impressions when you awake. No matter how odd they may seem, eventually they can offer financial solutions.

PISCES

*The year ahead for those
born under the sign of the Fish*
February 19–March 20

A touch of poetry and gentility surrounds the Fish. Swimming quietly through the waters of life, a veil of secrecy and inaccessibility is present. The image of two Fish linked yet pulling in opposite directions hints at great duality, ingenuity, and creativity. Neptune-ruled Pisces is receptive and emotional, yet often a bit melancholy and retiring, especially if others are harsh or surroundings grow stressful.

Spring begins with a holding pattern, as Mars opposes you. Postponements by another cause delays. Mercury hovers in your sign completing a retrograde cycle on April 16. Revise and suggest alternatives. During the last half of April when companions are more decisive, it's easier to complete projects or fulfill an obligation. On May Eve bless a pen that appeals to you. Affirm that this magical writing implement will seal your signature with blessings. Use it whenever you finalize contracts or agreements in the future.

The mutable sign eclipses on May 20 and June 4 highlight the important angular houses ruling family life and career in your chart. You'll juggle responsibilities and changing circumstances linked to both areas during the weeks before the summer solstice. A flexible outlook helps you make needed adjustments. Vacation travel is favored June 8 – 25 when Mercury dashes through your 5th house of leisure and pleasure. It's also a great influence for problem solving and sharing ideas.

Pressures lessen in early July. The Sun beams a benevolent influence through your sister water sign of Cancer until July 22. At Lammas devote ritual work to illuminating that which is hidden. Throughout August Mercury emphasizes your wellness sector. Seek information about health concerns; those of a precious pet can be of interest too. On August 31 the Blue Moon shines in your sign while conjoining Neptune. Ask your guardian angel for assistance. Near the autumnal equinox help will arrive. A kindly stranger or reliable friend can play a role in facilitating the angelic intervention.

Late summer and early autumn welcome positive Mars and Mercury transits through your 9th house. A journey to admire colorful foliage or a stop at a local farm for organic produce will rejuvenate you. Mid-October is a perfect time to finalize plans related to higher education. Just before Samhain Venus turns sultry while crossing into your 8th house. Through November 21 you'll be devoted to the quest for deeper intimacy through a meaningful relationship. The Scorpio eclipse on November 13 occurs as Neptune turns direct in your sign. This supportive celestial pattern helps you transcend obstacles and realize your heart's desire.

December finds Uranus completing a retrograde in your money sector.

You'll feel a greater sense of freedom; a debt or other financial obligation is easier to cope with or is resolved. December 1 – 15: Venus and Saturn send good financial energies your way. Expect a holiday bonus or other unexpected funds. Pluto, the Sun, Mercury, and Venus assemble in your 11th house during January. Politics, charitable endeavors, and community life fascinate. New associates impress you with their different outlooks near the New Moon on January 11. Some of your previously held ideas are changing.

By Candlemas the energy shifts. You'll grow bored with crowds and group dynamics. Graciously retreating to spend time in quiet contemplation, you'll prefer to nurture a relationship of substance near Valentine's Day. On February 26 Venus enters your sign and quickly conjoins Neptune in your 1st house. A charismatic quality emanates from you throughout the rest of the winter. Near your birthday there might be an opportunity to dance for an audience, perform music, or audition for a role in a theatrical production. Strive to project your most desirable image to the outer world. Influential people notice you, ushering in opportunities.

HEALTH

Often those born under the sign of the Fish enjoy adding an aquarium to the home or workplace. This emits a beneficial, healing energy. Another type of water feature can be substituted. Place it at the Feng Shui compass point corresponding to an area of the body in need of healing (north–ears, northeast– hands, east–feet, southeast–lower back and legs, south–eyes, southwest–internal body cavities, west–mouth and teeth, northwest–brain).

LOVE

From early April until August 7 Venus makes a tense aspect; your sector of home and family is the pivot point. Family obligations or personality clashes with relatives can pose some stumbling blocks for a romance. Patience is a must while trying to balance the different kinds of love and loyalty in your life. Hold on — the last three weeks of August, the first half of December, and late February bring promising star patterns for true love.

SPIRITUALITY

Intense Pluto is your spiritual and esoteric ruler. Since Pluto provides a cosmic link to the afterlife, a near-death experience or past life regression can enhance your spiritual awakening. "I leave the Father's home and turning back I save" is your spiritual mission statement. You offer spiritual awakening to those who were once left behind. The November 13 eclipse falls in your sector of spirituality, marking a significant time of spiritual progress.

FINANCE

Meticulous Virgo is your Earth sign and security source. Getting organized, meeting the details of daily obligations, and problem solving create security. While fulfilling the needs of others, you acquire all you seek. The celestial financial indicators are promising in late August–early October and in March, near your birthday.

The Tarot Sun

Lord of the Fire of the World

TAROT cards first developed in Italy during the middle of the fifteenth century as a game similar to whist, for three or four players. The pack consisted of four "pip" suits of the regular Italian deck – coins, batons, cups and swords which are akin to the diamonds, clubs, hearts and spades of our standard decks, to which had been added a fifth suit known as "triumphs" or "trumps". These consisted of twenty-one allegorical images, later numbered and named, plus a single unnumbered one, making seventy-eight cards in all.

In the game of Tarot, higher cards or trumps beat lower ones. Simply put, the game consisted of trying to win tricks by artfully playing the cards in your hand – always following suit – or if you could not follow suit, by playing a trump, which would "triumph" over an ordinary pip card. Whoever took the greatest number of tricks containing the largest number of significant cards was the winner. If a high trump was led and you wished to protect a lower one that you held, you could sacrificially play the 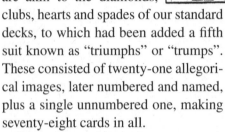 unnumbered "Fool" trump, although he would not be counted in your opponent's tricks. As described by an anonymous sixteenth century Italian writer, the Fool was considered to be captain of the first fifteen trumps: he could replace any other card during play, but he did not capture, nor was he ever captured – a notion which in itself seems to carry mystical implications.

The game of Tarot quickly became popular throughout Europe, and by the sixteenth century decks were being manufactured in France as well as Italy. The trump cards of regional French decks referred to nowadays as the Marseille Pattern are a mixed collection of Christian and Pagan images typical of the late Middle Ages. They quite apparently illustrate in some manner the story of the soul's progress through life into the afterlife.

The image of the Sun always arrives late in the trump sequence, generally numbered nineteen. It follows the Moon but precedes the second-to-last trump, Judgment, a card illustrating the great cosmic reckoning where, summoned by archangels, the ultimate fate of the soul is decided, a notion common to a variety of religions besides Christianity. The final trump is of course Eternity itself, often labeled the World.

Maybe because of their potent imagery, we find Tarot cards mentioned as a sortilege device in Italy within a century of their appearance, although they only take center stage as a tool of popular divination in the late eighteenth century. The same anonymous author who described the Fool's status also provides us with a glimpse of how the Tarot may have been interpreted by early cartomancers. He dubs the unknown creator of the cards "prudent", and describes how the four suits – coins, swords, maces (batons) and cups – represent the gaining of riches, the use of arms, literature and science, and pleasure. To these he adds the twenty-two trumps which he describes as "hieroglyphic", and believes are named "triumphs" because they affect the passions that triumph over humanity. Furthermore the writer believes the first fifteen trumps together with the four suits illustrate the "active life" of humanity, whereas the last six trumps describe the contemplative life that ends in Deity: "We rise with our eyes and intellects to the Heavens [the Tower], the Star, the Moon, the Sun, the supernatural creatures of God [Judgment], and the World [Eternity]," he writes, surely a Neoplatonic idea if ever there was one.

In all Tarot Sun cards, the solar orb or sunburst is prominently displayed. In the painted deck designed for the Milanese Visconti Sforzas, it is carried by a child or *putto*, possibly a youthful Mithras, Phaethon, or simply the sun god Apollo himself. Frequently the Sun's face is surrounded by a fiery nimbus, and beyond that, what appear to be drops of water, maybe water drawn up, later to fall as rain. The Sun trump of the Marseille Pattern and its derivative decks invariably depicts two children standing beneath the orb, possibly the card makers' representation of the fifth house of the horoscope, the House of Children and Pleasure, traditionally "ruled" by Leo and the sun. Using a fifteenth century astrologer's interpretation of the fifth house as a guide then, we can interpret it as a promise of good health, a heightening of creative powers, abundant joy, and maybe quite literally, children. The mage Arthur Edward Waite, who devised the popular Rider-Waite Tarot deck with Pamela Colman Smith in 1909, came to a similar conclusion regarding the Sun's meaning in divination: "material happiness, fortunate marriage, contentment". So feel happy when the Sun shows up in your spread; even when it appears reversed. It portends the same, and its radiance is said to illuminate all the cards about it. Definitely a win-win situation, and one of the best cards in the deck.

– PAUL HUSON

THE SUN.

More information on the Sun Tarot is available on line at http://TheWitchesAlmanac.com/AlmanacExtras/.

Sites of Awe
Travels through the Middle Kingdom, China

CHINA IS a country of rare treasures, many of which the Westerner is only able to see through books or films. In the spring of 2011, I was fortunate enough to visit several cities in central Eastern China. Here, I came face to face with Buddhist temples which would change the way my soul would breathe. The Lingyin Temple ("Temple of the Soul's Retreat"), for instance, is located in northwest Hangzhou in Zhejiang Province. The monastery was founded in 328 CE.

As our car pulls into the parking lot, I can already smell the scent of sweet incense in the air. We travel up a walkway to purchase tickets to the temple. Entrance fees, as well as gift shop sales, contribute to the upkeep, care and maintenance of the numerous buildings and extended grounds. The Lingyin Temple is one of the largest and wealthiest Buddhist temples in China, comprised of a multitude of pagodas and grottoes.

Temple of the Medicine Buddha

As we pass the grottos, I can almost see the faces of the Buddha reacting to my every move and thought – a smile, a gesture of compassion, a feeling of hope and joy. The path continues to a more central location surrounded by buildings containing images of the Buddha and bodhisattvas. The images are set in massive scale. Gold leaf, ornate painting and fine adornments surround the visitor. There are kneeling cushions in saffron and other traditional colors. Many people are lighting incense and praying before the statues. The manner of prayer distinguishes the novice from the experienced devotee. You also witness differences in prayer style, depending on the home or previous experience of each visitor. While here, one of my native Chinese guides teaches me a traditional Tibetan method of Buddhist prayer.

The first building I enter is the temple of Bhaisajyaguru Buddha, commonly called the Medicine Buddha. Here, when I close my eyes and stand before this enormous statue, I feel open and know that healing energy is pouring into me – exactly what I need. The pains that visitors arrive with – whether physical, emotional, mental or spiritual – are washed away by the timeless, infinite compassion of the Bhaisajyaguru Buddha.

Guan Yin and the
Hall of the Five Hundred Arhats

The second and most important hall is the Grand Hall of the Great Sage, which stands almost 110 feet tall and houses a statue of the Shakyamuni Buddha. Carved of camphor wood, it is the largest wooden Buddhist statue in China. This awe-inspiring image takes away all sense of time and separation. I feel like I am a part of every person who has ever seen this statue or experienced the nature of the Buddha. As if this was not overwhelming enough, I begin to circle round the back of the statue at the opposite side of the building and come face to face with a statue of Guan Yin, behind which is a colossal backdrop that details carved images of approximately 150 Buddhist personas. I stand before her image, which is nearly 100 feet tall. I am instantly showered in music, art, beauty, compassion and inner strength, the likes of which I have never before known.

Catching my breath once more, I enter the Hall of Five Hundred Arhats where I am loomed over by five hundred elevated, larger than life-size bronze images of the Buddha in every aspect of humanity imaginable. The building has a complex floor plan. At the centre of the building stands a bronze canopy housing statues of four bodhisattvas representing the four great cardinal

directions of the world. This is currently the tallest solid bronze structure in the world. I take several minutes to greet each image and feel the surge of power that the presence of each inspires within me.

This temple is far more than I had ever expected to experience. At every turn, there is another image, another bodhisattva, another symbol and each time I am overwhelmed. I am spiritually moved in a profound way. The opening of the lotus brings new meaning to my inner self. Being surrounded by hundreds of dedicated visitors and monks praying, chanting, studying and meditating creates an atmosphere that brings heaven to earth. Words cannot explain the intense feeling of honor and pride in just being myself and being alive in this truly sacred place.

– ARMAND TABER

Images can be seen at www.TheWitches Almanac.com/magicalsites2

Reviews

Old World Witchcraft: A Grimoire of the Magical Ways from Ancient to Modern Times by Raven Grimassi
ISBN: 9781578635054
Paperback, Weiser Books
6x9, 272 pages, 30 B&W Images
October 1, 2011

THE CULMINATION of decades of research, Raven Grimassi's *Old World Witchcraft* is an engaging search for the true historical figure of the witch. Troubled by the mainstream academic portrayal of the witch as consort of the devil and the sabbat as a blasphemy against the Christian mass, Grimassi challenges accepted historical sources and makes a compelling case for the consideration of more esoteric ones. The breadth of information presented is staggering: from ancient folklore to modern academic treatise, from Renaissance art to Neo-Pagan practices, Grimassi conceivably leaves no source unexamined to uncover the Old Ways Witch. Using the tools of the historian, anthropologist, and linguist, Grimassi peals back layers of misconception and prejudice to reveal a portrait of the witch not as evil hag but as an ordinary person in commune with the forest, steeped in an enchanted worldview.

In addition to being a quest for the unvarnished witch, *Old World Witchcraft* is an examination of how the Old Ways continue to be practiced today. Grimassi does not argue for a lineage of witchcraft traceable from antiquity to present unbroken. Instead, he explores how the Old Ways are elementally reinvented over and over to become both new and ancient. The last half of the book is a practical manual to how the Old Ways are practiced today. A modern grimoire, it touches on subjects from the consecration and ritual use of sacred tools to the use of plants in magic as well as instructions to calling on deities. *Old World Witchcraft* functions as a comprehensive yet open ended introduction to a modern practice and its ancient origins.

The Moon and the Night Spirit
Of Dreams Forgotten and Fables Untold
Digipak CD 2005,
Equilibrium Music

Hungarian folk duo The Moon and the Night Spirit sing of haunting fairy tales and mystical journeys, bringing a rare air of authenticity to their art. The title of their debut album, *Of Dreams*

Forgotten and Fables Untold (2005), describes their repertoire perfectly. The band describes their work as etherial sylvan music. This first album includes several songs sung in English, while their follow-up albums, *Rego Redtem*, *Offorras*, and the newest offering, *Mohalepte*, are primarily in their native tongue. The language barrier doesn't matter though because their songs are soundscapes that evoke inner emotions beyond words. If you like Omnia and Faun then you will love The Moon and the Night Spirit.

Pandemonaeon
Dangerous Beauty
www.pandemonaeon.net

Self-described as Gothic Tribal Folk Metal, this band came into being as a collaboration between San Francisco Celtic Pagan artist Sharon Knight and German guitarist Winter. Combining Middle Eastern, Scandinavian, and Celtic folk influences with modern rock styling, Pandemonaeon is not your fluffy bunny type folk experience. This is the music of cold hard steel blending with the tender tones of delight. This music epitomizes the traditional saying: "The brightest light shines forth from the darkest shadow". Be prepared to be excited, but expect to be guilt-free afterwards. Pandemonaeon recently performed live at the annual California event PantheaCon. Reportedly a raucous good-time was had by all.

Numbers Game

Is a five-leaf clover lucky? Luckier than a four leaf clover?

– Caseday M.
Medford, OR

We all know that the rare four leaf clover is inherently lucky. If one finds a four leaf clover he or she can expect to encounter a new lover, gain protection from evil charms, or discover once invisible faery folk. But there is less consensus on the virtues of the five leaf clover, an even rarer spectacle than its quatrefoil cousin. Some believe that the five leaf clover is especially fortunate and portends monetary gain. However, others believe the bad luck contained in a five leaf clover is so potent that the offending plant must be burned immediately. Of course, still others contend that the five leaf clover is nothing more than a genetically mutated common clover and has nothing to do with luck, only with probability.

La Muerte Dulce

Loved the article in last year's Almanac about the Day of the Dead. It has inspired me to throw a "dia de los muertos" party for my children and their friends instead of indulging them yet again in Halloween's mad grab for candy. The article gave me lots of ideas on what to cook but not a whole lot on what to do. Any thoughts?

– Maureen P.
Austin, TX

Dia de los Muertos is as much a celebration of the creative energies of the living as of the dead. Use your party as an opportunity for some hands-on activities. Here is one simple project to get you started: Paper flowers, for decorating your altar. All you need are some pipe cleaners and brightly colored tissue paper. Take several squares of paper and layer them together. Fold each layer over in an accordion pattern. Wrap the top of a pipe cleaner around the middle of the folded layers, pulling the bottom portion down to create the stem. Carefully pull the layers of paper up, starting from the middle, to create the petals. Once you get the hang of this simple structure, try experimenting with different folding techniques to create unique flower patterns.

Sites of Awe

I have a question for Armand Taber. Can you suggest a family vacation site in the United States that would incorporate sacred sites? Somewhere off the beaten path?

– Joshua B.
Cache, OK

America abounds in notable sites of awe, from the expanse of the Grand Canyon to the cascades of Niagara Falls to the Great Trees of Pacific Northwest (featured in last years Almanac). But America is also home to lesser known sacred sites, like the Serpent Mound in Ohio, "Mystery Hill" (otherwise known as America's Stonehenge) in New Hampshire, or Devil's Tower in Wyoming. Try exploring your local surroundings – you may be surprised at the sacred sites hiding in your own back yard.

Attractive Opposites

I heard there was an easy way for figuring out the zodiac sign of the full moon in any given month, but can't remember. Can you help?

– Brian T.
e-mail

The full moon is transiting the zodiac sign directly opposite the current sun sign. For the non-astrologers among us, simply determine the current sun sign, then count six signs forward. (In the correct order, of course!) For example, if the sun is in Aries, the moon is in Libra. If the sun is in Aquarius, the moon is in Leo.

Star Light, Star Bright

My young niece is starting to ask questions about witchcraft. What is an age appropriate way to introduce her to spellwork? She is 5 years old.

– Ravenbrook
e-mail

Some of the earliest spells we learn are as children, in the form of nursery rhymes. Your niece may already know some spells. "Star light, star bright, first star I see tonight – I wish I may,

I wish I might, have the wish I wish tonight" might very well be the first spell we learn. Other common nursery rhymes also have magical connotations. "Rain rain go away, come again some other day; Little (insert name) wants to play" is likely our first attempt at weather magic. Look through a book of nursery rhymes and see what other spells you can find together!

Let us hear from you, too

We love to hear from our readers. Letters should be sent with the writer's name (or just first name or initials), address, daytime phone number and e-mail address, if available. Published material may be edited for clarity or length. All letters and e-mails will become the property of The Witches' Almanac Ltd. and will not be returned. We regret that due to the volume of correspondence we cannot reply to all communications.

The Witches' Almanac, Ltd.
P.O. Box 1292
Newport, RI 02840-9998
info@TheWitchesAlmanac.com
www.TheWitchesAlmanac.com

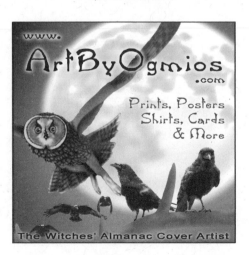

The products and services offered above are paid advertisements.

A NEW LOOK at the OLD WORLD
from WEISER BOOKS

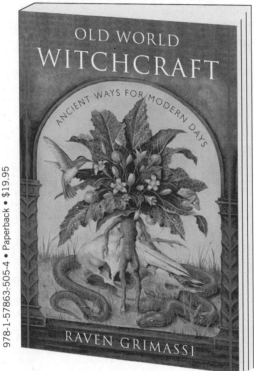

978-1-57863-505-4 • Paperback • $19.95

Noted author Raven Grimassi covers new terrain in *Old World Witchcraft* "an enchanted worldview." Providing a magical view of the Plant Kingdom (the "Old World") and the spirits attached to it, Grimassi reveals rarely discussed topics such as the concept of Shadow as the organic memory of the earth and he provides methods for interfacing with it to derive empowerment directly from the ancient source. *Old World Witchcraft* is for people who want to take the next step and are eager for the more rooted ways that have remained largely hidden.

To view a complete list of new and related titles log onto *www.redwheelweiser.com*

Weiser Books
Available wherever books and ebooks are sold.
www.redwheelweiser.com • P: 800.423.7087 • orders@redwheelweiser.com

The Witchcraft of Dame Darrel of York

Charles Godfrey Leland

Introduction by Robert Mathiesen

The Witches' Almanac presents:

- *A previously unpublished work by folklorist Charles Godfrey Leland.*
- *Published in full color facsimile with a text transcript.*
- *Forward by Prof. Robert Mathiesen.*

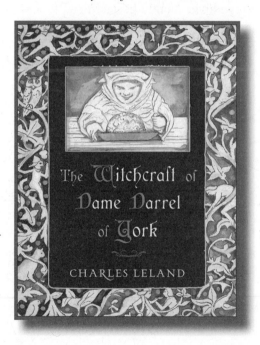

This beautifully reproduced facsimile of the illuminated manuscript will shed light on an ancient tradition as well as provide the basis for a modern practice. It will be treasured by those practicing Pagans, scholars, and all those fascinated by the legend and lore of England.

Standard hardcover edition ($65.00).
Deluxe numbered edition with slipcase ($85.00).
Exclusive full leather bound, numbered and slip cased edition ($145.00).

For further information visit http://thewitchesalmanac.com/damedarrel.html

The HORNED SHEPHERD
by EDGAR JEPSON

Woodcuts by WILFRED JONES

WANDER THE MAGICAL WORLD of the Valley of Fine
Fleeces with a fascinating cast of characters. Meet Big Anna,
keeper of both the pagan flame and Cross; a Princess aflame
for a strange lover; an Egyptian Priest, steward of mysteries;
Friar Paul, lean and sinister; and Saccabe the Black Goat,
Father of Many Flocks. Above all you will encounter the mysterious Shepherd
of supernatural radiance, among whose curls nestle two small soft horns. Events
converge in the forest on Midsummer Eve at full moon as celebrants arrive with
meat, bread and wine for the Feast. The Wise Ones recognize the Horned Shepherd
as an ancient fertility god who should be sacrificed to enrich the land. Beautiful
woodcuts enhance the 146-page book. $16.95

❃ Newly expanded classics! ❧

The ABC of Magic Charms
Elizabeth Pepper

SINCE THE DAWN of mankind, an obscure instinct in the
human spirit has sought protection from mysterious forces
beyond mortal control. Human beings sought benefaction in the
three realms that share Earth with us — animal, mineral, vegetable. All three, humanity discovered, contain mysterious properties discovered over millennia through occult divination. An
enlarged edition of *Magic Charms from A to Z*, compiled by the
staff of *The Witches' Almanac*. $12.95

The Little Book of Magical Creatures
Elizabeth Pepper and Barbara Stacy

A loving tribute to the animal kingdom

AN UPDATE of the classic *Magical Creatures*, featuring Animals Tame, Animals Wild, Animals Fabulous – plus an added
section of enchanting animal myths from other times, other
places. *A must for all animal lovers.* $12.95

✤ a lady shape-shifts into a white doe
✤ two bears soar skyward
✤ Brian Boru rides a wild horse
✤ a wolf growls dire prophecy

ARADIA
GOSPEL OF THE WITCHES
Charles Godfrey Leland

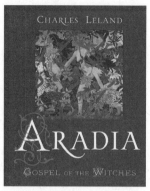

ARADIA IS THE FIRST work in English in which witchcraft is portrayed as an underground old religion, surviving in secret from ancient pagan times.

• Used as a core text by many modern neo-pagans.

• Foundation material containing traditional witchcraft practices

• This special edition features appreciations by such authors and luminaries as Paul Huson, Raven Grimassi, Judika Illes, Michael Howard, Christopher Penczak, Myth Woodling, Christina Oakley Harrington, Patricia Della-Piana, Jimahl di Fiosa and Donald Weiser. A beautiful and compelling work, this edition has brought the format up to date, while keeping the text unchanged. 172 pages $16.95

Available from Olympian Press...

Olympian Press, PO Box 29182, Providence, RI 02909 • www.OlympianPress.com

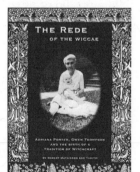

The Rede of the Wiccae
Adriana Porter, Gwen Thompson
and the Birth of a Tradition of Witchcraft
by Robert Mathiesen and Theitic

This is a tale told by Gwen Thompson about her grandmother, Adriana Porter, and how she came to be the last carrier of her ancestral Tradition of Witchcraft.

$22.95 plus $4.00 S & H — 200 pages
Available at OlympianPress.com/rede.html

Keepers of the Flame
Interviews with Elders of
Traditional Witchcraft in America
by Morganna Davies and Aradia Lynch

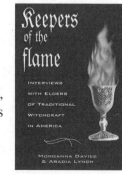

This book is not about the Elders, it is a record of their opinions, views, comments and ideas of what the Craft was, what it is today, and what they think it will be in the future.

$20.95 plus $4.00 S & H — 216 pages
Available at OlympianPress.com/keepers.html

Witches All

A Treasury from past editions...

Perfect for study or casual reading, Witches All *is a collection from* The Witches' Almanac *publications of the past. Arranged by topics, the book, like the popular almanacs, is thought provoking and often spurs me on to a tangent leading to even greater discovery. The information and art in the book – astrological attributes, spells, recipes, history, facts & figures is a great reminder of the history of the Craft, not just in recent years, but in the early days of the Witchcraft Revival in this century: the witch in an historical and cultural perspective.* Ty Bevington, Circle of the Wicker Man, Columbus, Ohio

Absolutely beautiful! I recently ordered Witches All *and I have to say I wasn't disappointed. The artwork and articles are first rate and for a longtime* Witches' Almanac *fan, it is a wonderful addition to my collection.* Witches' Almanac *devotees and newbies alike will love this latest effort. Very worth getting.*
Tarot3, Willits, California

GREEK GODS IN LOVE

Barbara Stacy casts a marvelously original eye on the beloved stories of Greek deities, replete with amorous oddities and escapades. We relish these tales in all their splendor and antic humor, and offer an inspired storyteller's fresh version of the old, old mythical magic.

MAGIC CHARMS FROM A TO Z

A treasury of amulets, talismans, fetishes and other lucky objects compiled by the staff of *The Witches' Almanac*. An invaluable guide for all who respond to the call of mystery and enchantment.

LOVE CHARMS

Love has many forms, many aspects. Ceremonies performed in witchcraft celebrate the joy and the blessings of love. Here is a collection of love charms to use now and ever after.

MAGICAL CREATURES

Mystic tradition grants pride of place to many members of the animal kingdom. Some share our life. Others live wild and free. Still others never lived at all, springing instead from the remarkable power of human imagination.